F25/45

KU-359-140

IF I HAD ONLY ONE SERMON TO PREACH

IF I HAD ONLY ONE SERMON TO PREACH

BY

THE ARCHBISHOP OF ARMAGH
RT. REV. GEO. H. MORRISON, D.D.
REV. A. E. GARVIE, D.D.
THE BISHOP OF WINCHESTER
REV. R. J. CAMPBELL, D.D.
MISS A. MAUDE ROYDEN
REV. W. E. ORCHARD, D.D.
REV. J. SCOTT LIDGETT, D.D.
THE BISHOP OF LONDON
REV. F. B. MEYER, D.D.
VERY REV. W. R. INGE, D.D.
REV. WHEELER ROBINSON, D.D.
THE BISHOP OF GLOUCESTER
REV. P. N. WAGGETT, D.D.
REV. JOHN A. HUTTON, D.D.
REV. H. R. L. SHEPPARD, C.H., D.D.
REV. STUDDERT KENNEDY, M.A.
REV. L. P. JACKS, D.D.
REV. F. W. NORWOOD, D.D.
REV. JAMES MOFFATT, D.D.

EDITED BY

SIR JAMES MARCHANT, K.B.E., LL.D.

CASSELL & COMPANY, LTD.
LONDON, TORONTO, MELBOURNE, & SYDNEY

1928

First Published 1928

PRINTED IN GREAT BRITAIN

PREFACE

A FEW sentences uttered nearly two thousand years ago by the Lord Himself, and chosen out of the four Gospels, appear as an Introduction to this volume. It is the Word which must be preached in every nation to every creature until the fullness of the time shall have come. They are followed by the messages of twenty of His witnesses, who have been commissioned to interpret and apply His Gospel, each in his or her own manner, to our day and generation. They have endeavoured to expound that aspect of the Word of the Lord which they would have chosen if they had had only one sermon to preach. All have hesitated, as well they might, before accepting the invitation. But in the end, they have settled upon their theme without serious misgiving. "I am glad," wrote one, "that you have imposed this hard task upon me." "It puts a preacher on his mettle," says another. "I have delivered such a sermon," writes a third; "perhaps it is the only sermon of which I have evidence that it has done no harm." One and all here preach their *one* sermon.

The reader will turn eagerly to the following pages to discover the themes chosen. A glance at the contents table will show that, although each contributor has written in ignorance of the choice of the others, they have fastened, almost with one accord, upon the greatest verities, the supreme quest of the soul, as one puts it—the vision, the love, the purposes, the trustworthiness, the "yea" and "nay" of God, as seen in Jesus Christ, His life and His Cross. After their own method they have attempted to interpret the Eternal Values so as to meet the needs of the halting and the hungry, the sinner and the saint, the sick and the weary, the challenge of science and the claim to happiness ; for the preachers have in mind the desires of youth, the disillusions of age, the problems of the hour, the ups and downs of this troublous life, and the necessity of re-presenting the Gospel message in the language of their times.

Hear, again, the Word of the Lord, uttered now as of old, old yet ever new, which He who was the Word and the Incarnation thereof commissioned His disciples going into all the world to preach to every creature, and of which it is said, " It shall not return unto Him void, but it shall accomplish that whereunto He sent it."

J. M.

Advent, 1927.

CONTENTS

Contents

PROLOGUE

In the beginning was the Word.
And the Word was with God.
And the Word was God.

THE WORD OF THE LORD

"*Heaven and earth shall pass away, but my words shall not pass away.*"

I

AND seeing the multitudes, Jesus went up into a mountain: and when he was set, his disciples came unto him: and he opened his mouth, and taught them, saying,

Blessed are the poor in spirit: for their's is the kingdom of heaven.

Blessed are they that mourn: for they shall be comforted.

Blessed are the meek: for they shall inherit the earth.

Blessed are they which do hunger and thirst after righteousness: for they shall be filled.

Blessed are the merciful: for they shall obtain mercy.

Blessed are the pure in heart: for they shall see God.

Blessed are the peacemakers: for they shall be called the children of God.

Blessed are they which are persecuted for righteousness' sake: for their's is the kingdom of heaven.

Blessed are ye, when men shall revile you, and persecute you, and shall say all manner of evil against you falsely for my sake.

Rejoice, and be exceeding glad: for great is your reward in heaven: for so persecuted they the prophets which were before you.

Lay not up for yourselves treasures upon earth, where moth and rust doth corrupt, and where thieves break through and steal:

But lay up for yourselves treasures in heaven, where neither moth nor rust doth corrupt, and where thieves do not break through nor steal:

For where your treasure is, there will your heart be also.

The light of the body is the eye: if therefore thine eye be single, thy whole body shall be full of light.

But if thine eye be evil, thy whole body shall be full of darkness. If therefore the light that is in thee be darkness, how great is that darkness!

No man can serve two masters: for either he will hate the one, and love the other; or else he will hold to the one, and despise the other. Ye cannot serve God and mammon.

Take heed that ye do not your alms before men, to be seen of them: otherwise ye have no reward of your Father which is in heaven.

Therefore when thou doest thine alms, do not sound a trumpet before thee, as the hypocrites do in the synagogues and in the streets, that they may have glory of men. Verily I say unto you, They have their reward.

But when thou doest alms, let not thy left hand know what thy right hand doeth:

That thine alms may be in secret: and thy Father which seeth in secret himself shall reward thee openly.

And when thou prayest, thou shalt not be as the hypocrites are: for they love to pray standing in the synagogues and in the corners of the streets, that they may be seen of men. Verily I say unto you, They have their reward.

But thou, when thou prayest, enter into thy closet, and when thou hast shut thy door, pray to thy Father which is in secret; and thy Father which seeth in secret shall reward thee openly.

But when ye pray, use not vain repetitions, as the heathen do: for they think that they shall be heard for their much speaking.

Be not ye therefore like unto them: for your Father knoweth what things ye have need of, before ye ask him.

After this manner therefore pray ye:

Our Father which art in heaven, Hallowed be thy name.

Thy kingdom come. Thy will be done in earth, as it is in heaven.

Give us this day our daily bread.

And forgive us our debts, as we forgive our debtors.

And lead us not into temptation, but deliver us from evil: For thine is the kingdom, and the power, and the glory, for ever. Amen.

For if ye forgive men their trespasses, your heavenly Father will also forgive you:

But if ye forgive not men their trespasses, neither will your Father forgive your trespasses.

Judge not, that ye be not judged.

For with what judgment ye judge, ye shall be judged: and with what measure ye mete, it shall be measured to you again.

And why beholdest thou the mote that is in thy brother's eye, but considerest not the beam that is in thine own eye?

Or how wilt thou say to thy brother, Let me pull out the mote out of thine eye; and, behold, a beam is in thine own eye?

Thou hypocrite, first cast out the beam out of thine own eye; and then shalt thou see clearly to cast out the mote out of thy brother's eye.

II

A certain man had two sons:

And the younger of them said to his father, Father, give me the portion of goods that falleth to me. And he divided unto them his living.

And not many days after the younger son gathered all together, and took his journey into a far country, and there wasted his substance with riotous living.

And when he had spent all, there arose a mighty famine in that land; and he began to be in want.

And he went and joined himself to a citizen of that country; and he sent him into his fields to feed swine.

And he would fain have filled his belly with the husks that the swine did eat: and no man gave unto him.

And when he came to himself, he said, How many hired servants of my father's have bread enough and to spare, and I perish with hunger!

I will arise and go to my father, and will say unto him, Father, I have sinned against heaven, and before thee,

And am no more worthy to be called thy son: make me as one of thy hired servants.

And he arose, and came to his father. But when he was yet a great way off, his father saw him, and had compassion, and ran, and fell on his neck, and kissed him.

And the son said unto him, Father, I have sinned against heaven, and in thy sight, and am no more worthy to be called thy son.

But the father said to his servants, Bring forth the best robe, and put it on him; and put a ring on his hand, and shoes on his feet:

And bring hither the fatted calf, and kill it; and let us eat, and be merry:

For this my son was dead, and is alive again; he was lost, and is found. And they began to be merry.

Now his elder son was in the field: and as he came and drew nigh to the house, he heard musick and dancing.

And he called one of the servants, and asked what these things meant.

And he said unto him, Thy brother is come; and thy father hath killed the fatted calf, because he hath received him safe and sound.

And he was angry, and would not go in: therefore came his father out, and intreated him.

And he answering said to his father, Lo, these many years do I serve thee, neither transgressed I at any time thy commandment: and yet thou never gavest me a kid, that I might make merry with my friends:

But as soon as this thy son was come, which hath devoured thy living with harlots, thou hast killed for him the fatted calf.

And he said unto him, Son, thou art ever with me, and all that I have is thine.

It was meet that we should make merry, and be glad: for this thy brother was dead, and is alive again; and was lost, and is found.

For the Son of man is come to save that which was lost.

How think ye ? if a man have an hundred sheep, and one of them be gone astray, doth he not leave the ninety and nine, and goeth into the mountains, and seeketh that which is gone astray ?

And if so be that he find it, verily I say unto you, he rejoiceth more of that sheep, than of the ninety and nine which went not astray.

Even so it is not the will of your Father which is in heaven, that one of these little ones should perish.

III

Enter ye in at the strait gate : for wide is the gate, and broad is the way, that leadeth to destruction, and many there be which go in thereat :

Because strait is the gate, and narrow is the way, which leadeth unto life, and few there be that find it.

Beware of false prophets, which come to you in sheep's clothing, but inwardly they are ravening wolves.

Ye shall know them by their fruits. Do men gather grapes of thorns, or figs of thistles ?

Even so every good tree bringeth forth good fruit ; but a corrupt tree bringeth forth evil fruit.

A good tree cannot bring forth evil fruit, neither can a corrupt tree bring forth good fruit.

Every tree that bringeth not forth good fruit is hewn down, and cast into the fire.

Wherefore by their fruits ye shall know them.

Not every one that saith unto me, Lord, Lord, shall enter into the kingdom of heaven ; but he that doeth the will of my Father which is in heaven.

A certain man went down from Jerusalem to Jericho,

and fell among thieves, which stripped him of his raiment, and wounded him, and departed, leaving him half dead.

And by chance there came down a certain priest that way: and when he saw him, he passed by on the other side.

And likewise a Levite, when he was at the place, came and looked on him, and passed by on the other side.

But a certain Samaritan, as he journeyed, came where he was: and when he saw him, he had compassion on him.

And went to him, and bound up his wounds, pouring in oil and wine, and set him on his own beast, and brought him to an inn, and took care of him.

And on the morrow when he departed, he took out two pence, and gave them to the host, and said unto him, Take care of him; and whatsoever thou spendest more, when I come again, I will repay thee.

Which now of these three, thinkest thou, was neighbour unto him that fell among the thieves?

And he said, He that showed mercy on him. Then said Jesus unto him, Go, and do thou likewise.

Which of you shall have a friend, and shall go unto him at midnight, and say into him, Friend, lend me three loaves:

For a friend of mine in his journey is come to me, and I have nothing to set before him?

And he from within shall answer and say, Trouble me not: the door is now shut, and my children are with me in bed; I cannot rise and give thee.

I say unto you, Though he will not rise and give him,

because he is his friend, yet because of his importunity he will rise and give him as many as he needeth.

And I say unto you, Ask, and it shall be given you; seek, and ye shall find; knock, and it shall be opened unto you.

For every one that asketh receiveth; and he that seeketh findeth; and to him that knocketh it shall be opened.

If a son shall ask bread of any of you that is a father, will he give him a stone? or if he ask a fish, will he for a fish give him a serpent?

Or if he shall ask an egg, will he offer him a scorpion?

If ye then, being evil, know how to give good gifts unto your children: how much more shall your heavenly Father give the Holy Spirit to them that ask him?

When the Son of man shall come in his glory, and all the holy angels with him, then shall he sit upon the throne of his glory:

And before him shall be gathered all nations: and he shall separate them one from another, as a shepherd divideth his sheep from the goats:

And he shall set the sheep on his right hand, but the goats on the left.

Then shall the King say unto them on his right hand, Come, ye blessed of my Father, inherit the kingdom prepared for you from the foundation of the world:

For I was an hungred, and ye gave me meat: I was thirsty, and ye gave me drink: I was a stranger, and ye took me in:

Naked, and ye clothed me: I was sick, and ye visited me: I was in prison, and ye came unto me.

Then shall the righteous answer him, saying, Lord,

when saw we thee an hungred, and fed thee? or thirsty, and gave thee drink?

When saw we thee a stranger, and took thee in? or naked, and clothed thee?

Or when saw we thee sick, or in prison, and came unto thee?

And the King shall answer and say unto them, Verily I say unto you, Inasmuch as ye have done it unto one of the least of these my brethren, ye have done it unto me.

Then shall he say also unto them on the left hand, Depart from me, ye cursed, into everlasting fire, prepared for the devil and his angels:

For I was an hungred, and ye gave me no meat: I was thirsty, and ye gave me no drink:

I was a stranger, and ye took me not in: naked, and ye clothed me not: sick, and in prison, and ye visited me not.

Then shall they also answer him, saying, Lord, when saw we thee an hungred, or athirst, or a stranger, or naked, or sick, or in prison, and did not minister unto thee?

Then shall he answer them saying, Verily I say unto you, Inasmuch as ye did it not to one of the least of these, ye did it not to me.

IV

It is written, Man shall not live by bread alone, but by every word that proceedeth out of the mouth of God.

I am the bread of life: he that cometh to me shall never hunger; and he that believeth on me shall never thirst.

Verily, verily, I say unto you, He that believeth on me hath everlasting life.

I am the bread of life.

Your fathers did eat manna in the wilderness, and are dead.

This is the bread which cometh down from heaven, that a man may eat thereof, and not die.

I am the living bread which came down from heaven: if any man eat of this bread, he shall live for ever: and the bread that I will give is my flesh, which I will give for the life of the world.

It is the spirit that quickeneth; the flesh profiteth nothing: the words that I speak unto you, they are spirit, and they are life.

The ground of a certain rich man brought forth plentifully:

And he thought within himself, saying, What shall I do, because I have no room where to bestow my fruits?

And he said, This will I do: I will pull down my barns, and build greater; and there will I bestow all my fruits and my goods.

And I will say to my soul, Soul, thou hast much goods laid up for many years; take thine ease, eat, drink, and be merry.

But God said unto him, Thou fool, this night thy soul shall be required of thee: then whose shall those things be which thou hast provided?

So is he that layeth up treasure for himself, and is not rich toward God.

And he said unto his disciples, Therefore I say unto

you, Take no thought for your life, what ye shall eat; neither for the body, what ye shall put on.

The life is more than meat, and the body is more than raiment.

Consider the ravens: for they neither sow nor reap; which neither have storehouse nor barn; and God feedeth them: how much more are ye better than the fowls?

And which of you with taking thought can add to his stature one cubit?

If ye then be not able to do that thing which is least, why take ye thought for the rest?

Consider the lilies how they grow: they toil not, they spin not; and yet I say unto you, that Solomon in all his glory was not arrayed like one of these.

If then God so clothe the grass, which is to day in the field, and to morrow is cast into the oven; how much more will he clothe you, O ye of little faith?

And seek not ye what ye shall eat, or what ye shall drink, neither be ye of doubtful mind.

For all these things do the nations of the world seek after: and your Father knoweth that ye have need of these things.

But rather seek ye the kingdom of God; and all these things shall be added unto you.

Fear not, little flock; for it is your Father's good pleasure to give you the kingdom.

V

Verily, verily, I say unto you, Except a man be born of water and of the Spirit, he cannot enter into the kingdom of God.

That which is born of the flesh is flesh; and that which is born of the Spirit is spirit.

Marvel not that I said unto thee, Ye must be born again.

The wind bloweth where it listeth, and thou hearest the sound thereof, but canst not tell whence it cometh, and whither it goeth: so is every one that is born of the Spirit.

Verily, verily, I say unto you, Except ye eat the flesh of the Son of man, and drink his blood, ye have no life in you.

Whoso eateth my flesh, and drinketh my blood, hath eternal life; and I will raise him up at the last day.

For my flesh is meat indeed, and my blood is drink indeed.

He that eateth my flesh, and drinketh my blood, dwelleth in me, and I in him.

As the living Father hath sent me, and I live by the Father: so he that eateth me, even he shall live by me.

This is that bread which came down from heaven: not as your fathers did eat manna, and are dead: he that eateth of this bread shall live for ever.

Doth this offend you?

Take, eat: this is my body. . . . This is my blood of the new testament, which is shed for many. Verily I say unto you, I will drink no more of the fruit of the vine, until that day that I drink it new in the kingdom of God.

I am the true vine, and my Father is the husbandman.

Every branch in me that beareth not fruit he taketh away: and every branch that beareth fruit, he purgeth it, that it may bring forth more fruit.

Now ye are clean through the word which I have spoken unto you.

Abide in me, and I in you. As the branch cannot bear fruit of itself, except it abide in the vine; no more can ye, except ye abide in me.

I am the vine, ye are the branches: He that abideth in me, and I in him, the same bringeth forth much fruit: for without me ye can do nothing.

If a man abide not in me, he is cast forth as a branch, and is withered; and men gather them, and cast them into the fire, and they are burned.

If ye abide in me, and my words abide in you, ye shall ask what ye will, and it shall be done unto you.

Herein is my Father glorified, that ye bear much fruit; so shall ye be my disciples.

As the Father hath loved me, so have I loved you: continue ye in my love.

If ye keep my commandments, ye shall abide in my love; even as I have kept my Father's commandments, and abide in his love.

These things have I spoken unto you, that my joy might remain in you, and that your joy might be full.

This is my commandment, That ye love one another, as I have loved you.

Greater love hath no man than this, that a man lay down his life for his friends.

Ye are my friends, if ye do whatsoever I command you.

Henceforth I call you not servants; for the servant knoweth not what his lord doeth: but I have called you friends; for all things that I have heard of my Father I have made known unto you.

Ye have not chosen me, but I have chosen you, and ordained you, that ye should go and bring forth fruit, and that your fruit should remain: that whatsoever ye shall ask of the Father in my name, he may give it to you.

These things I command you, that ye love one another.

If the world hate you, ye know that it hated me before it hated you.

If ye were of the world, the world would love his own: but because ye are not of the world, but I have chosen you out of the world, therefore the world hateth you.

Remember the word that I said unto you, The servant is not greater than his lord. If they have persecuted me, they will also persecute you; if they have kept my saying, they will keep your's also.

But all these things will they do unto you for my name's sake, because they know not him that sent me.

Verily, verily, I say unto you, He that believeth on me, the works that I do shall he do also; and greater works than these shall he do; because I go unto my Father.

And whatsoever ye shall ask in my name, that will I do, that the Father may be glorified in the Son.

If ye shall ask any thing in my name, I will do it.

If ye love me, keep my commandments.

And I will pray the Father, and he shall give you another Comforter, that he may abide with you for ever;

Even the Spirit of truth; whom the world cannot receive, because it seeth him not, neither knoweth him: but ye know him; for he dwelleth with you, and shall be in you.

I will not leave you comfortless: I will come to you.

Yet a little while, and the world seeth me no more; but ye see me: because I live, ye shall live also.

At that day ye shall know that I am in my Father, and ye in me, and I in you.

He that hath my commandments, and keepeth them, he it is that loveth me: and he that loveth me shall be loved of my Father, and I will love him, and will manifest myself to him.

I am the good shepherd, and know my sheep, and am known of mine.

As the Father knoweth me, even so know I the Father: and I lay down my life for the sheep.

And other sheep I have, which are not of this fold: them also I must bring, and they shall hear my voice; and there shall be one fold, and one shepherd.

Therefore doth my Father love me, because I lay down my life, that I might take it again.

No man taketh it from me, but I lay it down of myself. I have power to lay it down, and I have power to take it again. This commandment have I received of my Father.

Let not your heart be troubled: ye believe in God, believe also in me.

In my Father's house are many mansions: if it were not so, I would have told you. I go to prepare a place for you.

And if I go and prepare a place for you, I will come

again, and receive you unto myself; that where I am, there ye may be also.

And whither I go ye know, and the way ye know.

Thomas saith unto him, Lord, we know not whither thou goest; and how can we know the way?

Jesus saith unto him, I am the way, the truth, and the life: no man cometh unto the Father, but by me.

If ye had known me, ye should have known my Father also: and from henceforth ye know him, and have seen him.

He that believeth on me, believeth not on me, but on him that sent me.

And he that seeth me seeth him that sent me.

I am come a light into the world, that whosoever believeth on me should not abide in darkness.

And if any man hear my words, and believe not, I judge him not: for I came not to judge the world, but to save the world.

He that rejecteth me, and receiveth not my words, hath one that judgeth him: the word that I have spoken, the same shall judge him in the last day.

For I have not spoken of myself; but the Father which sent me, he gave me a commandment, what I should say, and what I should speak.

And I know that his commandment is life everlasting: whatsoever I speak therefore, even as the Father said unto me, so I speak.

My doctrine is not mine, but his that sent me.

If any man will do his will, he shall know of the doctrine, whether it be of God, or whether I speak of myself.

VI

Thou shalt love the Lord thy God with all thy heart, and with all thy soul, and with all thy mind.

This is the first and great commandment.

And the second is like unto it, Thou shalt love thy neighbour as thyself.

I am the light of the world: he that followeth me shall not walk in darkness, but shall have the light of life.

Come unto me, all ye that labour and are heavy laden, and I will give you rest.

Take my yoke upon you, and learn of me; for I am meek and lowly in heart: and ye shall find rest unto your souls.

For my yoke is easy, and my burden is light.

Whom do men say that I the Son of man am? And his disciples said, Some say that thou art John the Baptist; some, Elias; and others, Jeremias, or one of the prophets.

He saith unto them, But whom say ye that I am?

And Simon Peter answered and said, Thou art the Christ, the Son of the living God.

And Jesus answered and said into him, Blessed art thou, Simon Bar-jona: for flesh and blood hath not revealed it unto thee, but my Father which is in heaven. And I say also unto thee, That thou art Peter, and upon this rock I will build my church; and the gates of hell shall not prevail against it.

Peace be unto you: as my Father hath sent me, even so send I you.

Receive ye the Holy Ghost:

Whose soever sins ye remit, they are remitted unto them; and whose soever sins ye retain, they are retained.

All power is given unto me in heaven and in earth.

Go ye therefore, and teach all nations, baptizing them in the name of the Father, and of the Son, and of the Holy Ghost:

Teaching them to observe all things whatsoever I have commanded you: and, lo, I am with you alway, even unto the end of the world.

Heaven and earth shall pass away, but my words shall not pass away.

LOVE ETERNAL

THE ARCHBISHOP OF ARMAGH AND PRIMATE OF ALL IRELAND (THE MOST REV. CHARLES FREDERICK D'ARCY, M.A., D.D.)

Born in Dublin in 1859, *he is a member of an ancient Anglo-Norman family, seated for many centuries in co. Westmeath. First Science Scholar and Senior Moderator of Trinity College, Dublin, he obtained a first class in Divinity, and was ordained in* 1884. *As a clergyman he served for five years as a curate in Belfast, and for ten years in the rural parishes of Billy and Ballymana, in co. Antrim. In* 1900 *he became Vicar and Dean of Belfast, and in* 1903 *Bishop of Clogher. From Clogher he was translated to Ossory in* 1908, *and thence to Down in* 1911. *In* 1919 *he was elected Archbishop of Dublin, and in* 1920 *unanimously appointed Archbishop of Armagh and Primate of All Ireland. In* 1920 *he became Hon. D.D. of Oxford. He has been several times Select Preacher before the Universities of Dublin, Oxford, and Cambridge. He was Donnellan Lecturer in* 1897–8, *and again in* 1913–14*; also Liverpool Lecturer in* 1924*; in* 1927 *elected a Fellow of the British Academy. His published works include: "A Short Study of Ethics," used as a textbook in the Universities of London, Calcutta, etc., and translated into Japanese for use in Tokio; "Idealism and Theology;" "God and Freedom in Human Experience" (Donnellan Lectures), and "Science and Creation" (Liverpool Lectures).*

LOVE ETERNAL

BY THE ARCHBISHOP OF ARMAGH

"*Charity never faileth*": "*Love never faileth.*" *Or, to paraphrase the saying in the light of its context,* "*There is a Love which is Eternal.*"—1 Cor. xiii. 8.

A GREAT American essayist tells us that there are some people "who read God in a prose translation." They have never caught a glimpse of the Divine Vision, nor heard the cry of the seraphim, nor even felt the shaking of the temple. The wonder and the glory of heavenly things have never awakened their faculties to an answering recognition, much less stirred their souls to such a cry as that of the prophet of old: "Woe is me! for I am undone . . .: for mine eyes have seen the King, the Lord of Hosts."

As it was with Isaiah, so it was with the writers of the New Testament. The manifestation of God which had been given them in Jesus Christ, sweeter, higher, better even than that granted to the Old Testament seer, endowed them with the power to discern, not only the truth, but also the Divine splendour and beauty revealed to man in Him. Their spiritual capacities were enlarged, their faculties of apprehension and expression augmented.

This is notably true of the evangelists, and especially of St. Luke and St. John. It is also, and most eminently, characteristic of St. Paul. He tells us himself that he was caught up into Paradise and heard things which could not be uttered. But sometimes he saw and heard things which had to be uttered, but could not find expression in the language of ordinary speech.

There is a lyrical splendour about some passages in St. Paul's writings. So it is, for example, in the Epistle to the Romans (ch. viii), where he exhausts the power of language to express the nature of the love of God in Christ, from which no power can separate the trusting soul. So it is in the Epistle to the Philippians (ch. iii), where he chants a psalm of Christian progress. So it is also in the Second Epistle to the Corinthians (ch. vi), where with impetuous utterance he pours forth his experience of the pains and triumphs of his labours as a minister of Christ. But nowhere is this power of impassioned expression more vividly and more movingly displayed than in the description of love, or charity, which is known to us all as the thirteenth chapter of the First Epistle to the Corinthians.

This chapter, beginning with a strong emphasis on that virtue which was already a mark of the Christian community, soars higher and higher in language and thought until it becomes a veritable vision of God, a song of Divine Love. It is one of those passages, of which indeed there are many in Holy Scripture, which the sympathetic reader not only believes to have been inspired by the Spirit of God, but in which that inspiration is plainly manifested.

The word which is translated "charity" or "love" here, and elsewhere in the New Testament, is one which is not found in classical Greek. It is a word which Christianity created; or perhaps took over from the common speech, the current Greek of the Hellenised East, and endowed with a new and special significance. It was indeed one of the new things of the wonderful faith which Jesus Christ gave to men. And so we shall not go wrong if we regard this chapter as expressing an essential part of the new teaching, a message from heaven, central in the Gospel which the Apostles proclaimed. That will explain the fervour and exalted earnestness of St. Paul's language, as nothing else can.

In this lovely Psalm of Love the Apostle rises from his description of the "more excellent way," in which he desires all Christian people to walk, to the thought of Love in its perfection, as an eternal thing, Love as it is in God.

It is characteristic of St. Paul that, as he enlarges on any great theme, there comes to him, as in a flash, a sudden vision of some truth, arising out of the less exalted levels of thought on which he has been moving, and he is carried upward from earth to heaven. Many examples of this could be given from his writings. Here is a notable instance. "Love never faileth." In a moment the higher vision comes. Yes: it is eternal. Other things, even great things, change and pass away. Among the gifts which belonged to the Christian revelation and on which believing souls relied, and in which they rejoiced, were things which were yet fugitive in their nature. Prophecies, inspired teachings that is, cannot be for ever, because the prophet, the inspired teacher, speaks to his own age, in the language which belongs to it. His message is true and essential, but it is relative to a state of things which must pass. The gift of tongues was for an epoch only: it must cease. Knowledge, too, as we possess it, belongs to the imperfect order in which we now are; it will be lost in higher attainments. "For we know in part, and we prophesy in part: but when that which is perfect is come, that which is in part shall be done away. When I was a child, I spake as a child, I felt as a child, I thought as a child: now that I am become a man, I have put away childish things."

Here we are like children, grasping truth imperfectly, with faculties but partially developed; we are like those who dimly discern in some polished surface undefined shapes which we cannot fully comprehend. Such is our knowledge; such are our best teachings. The time of full revelation is reserved for the great future life. But one thing we know which is eternal, unfailing, unalterable in its quality: love—that Divine love which was manifested in Christ and given to His people as the rule of life. So we must, I believe, interpret these glowing words of St. Paul in which he sums up the thoughts of this great utterance.

What is love? Seldom do we ask ourselves that question. Perhaps it is well that we do not, for there is no question harder to answer. In the whole range of existence, material and spiritual, there is nothing more difficult to define. It is a great mystery. Perhaps it is the one final mystery. Some may doubt this assertion. If so, I am glad; for the doubt shows that their experience has overleapt their critical faculties. In some wonderful way they have been able to live what the intellect has not been able to explore. The fact is, they know as long as they do not inquire. They understand as long as they do not try to understand, like a great thinker of old who said of another mystery, "As long as you do not ask me, I know."

What is love? It is not knowledge; for it is not possible to know, in the scientific sense of the term, the soul of another. In every soul there is an unfathomable abyss. None can prove to demonstration the fidelity of a friend, or the love that is yet felt to be the surest fact of living. Again, love is not emotion. Our feelings, our emotions, come and go ; they change from day to day, from hour to hour. There are men and women who will go away into the heart of the Dark Continent, and give themselves for the souls of the heathen there, and yet it may be that their great love which involves the utmost sacrifice has not as much merely emotional force as the passion that many a youthful soul experiences and forgets in half a year. Yet one is great and heroic : the other trivial. No. Love is not emotion, though great emotions belong to it. Love owns feeling, but feeling is not love. Here is one of the marks which distinguish the love revealed by Christ from the merely human passion which, in our language, claims the same name.

St. John tells us that God is Love. It is a great revelation of the Divine Nature. It is also a great revelation of the nature of love—of the love which, as St. Paul teaches, is unfailing, eternal. I have said that you cannot know what love is, in the way of scientific knowledge. You can know it only by experience. But you can have great thoughts about it ; and one of the greatest of such thoughts is that God is Love. This is one of the greatest thoughts you can have about God—perhaps the very greatest. It is also, I think, the greatest thought you can have about love. For it means that love, being the very nature of God, is the greatest thing in the universe, and eternal.

Now, I think we can have other thoughts about love which will help us to see what all this means.

Our ordinary experience makes us think of material things as permanent and of spiritual things as fleeting. Men live and die and pass away. States, nations, races of men, live and die and pass away. But the great material world remains. It seems more enduring. The mountains stand to-day much as they stood thousands of years ago; they have been called "the everlasting hills." Rivers flow to the sea in their ancient courses: the Nile waters the Egypt of to-day as it watered the Egypt of the Pharaohs. Continents and islands are much the same now as they were when the Assyrians were lords of the East, or, later, when the Cæsars ruled their great Empire. Science, indeed, in these modern times has taught us that the great material world itself is in process of continual change. Yet how old it is compared with man and his works! But, through religious faith, has come to us a deeper thought. We have come to discern the reality of the unseen spiritual things. We have learned to discern our own souls within, and to believe there is in us that which can possess the gift of immortality.

Again, all material things, the mountains, rivers, islands, continents, the very world which includes them all, nay, the whole multitude of worlds, to the farthest bounds of space—all material things of whatsoever kind they be—are united, held together, in one great material universe. Now pass, once again, from the material to the spiritual, from the universe of matter to the whole multitude of spiritual beings. They too, all spirits, must be held together by some great bond of union. And what is that bond of union, that all-comprehending spiritual life? It is God. "In Him we live, and move, and have our being."

But when souls are united, when they are bound together in one, what do we call it ? Surely we call it Love.

Thus we can attain to some idea, however faint, of love as the nature of God and of love as eternal. It is that which gives unity, harmony, completeness, to the whole spiritual universe. And love is eternal, because it is the very essence of eternity.

We have seen that all spirits must be held in the arms of God's love. But what about the sinner ? Is he so held ? Yes, he is ; for if God let any man go, that moment he would perish. God is our life ; we cannot exist at all without Him. But the sinner is one who has opposed himself to that which is the very source of his life ; sin is lawlessness, division, the violation of love. Yet Divine Love does not let even the sinner go. "God so loved the world, that He gave His only begotten Son." The very heart and soul of those immortal words is that God has not let the world go, in spite of all the sin in it. He loves it still. And it is because of that love that it continues to exist. It is a very noteworthy fact that, throughout the New Testament, when atonement, reconciliation, is spoken of, it is always presented as the reconciliation of man to God, and not of God to man.

The very meaning of the Gospel of Christ is that all through the long ages of sin and shame the great Divine Eternal Love has persisted, never failing, never changing, never turning back because of human failure, never ceasing to work for the final overcoming of all evil and the perfecting of the Kingdom of God, which is the Kingdom of Love.

The central doctrines of Christianity are the Incarnation and the Atonement: God entering into human existence, and, incarnate, bearing the burden of our sin-stricken life, and passing through death for us. From the merely earthly point of view this wonderful Gospel story seems incredible. To the clever Greeks of old, as St. Paul tell us, it was foolishness. And so it is to many a clever mind to-day.

An old theologian used to say, "I believe because it is impossible:" certainly an amazing way of expressing the reason of his faith! But there was a profound truth underlying it; and here is that truth: What is impossible from the human point of view is entirely credible from the Divine point of view, because of God's exceeding greatness. It is only a low view of God's love which makes men think it incredible that the Divine Love should become incarnate, live a human life, and die upon the Cross. It is really because men's thoughts of God are so mean, so unworthy, that they think Him incapable of such a sacrifice. Is the Almighty not great enough, not noble enough, for such a thing?

There is a profound saying in the Epistle to the Hebrews which presents the truth to which we have attained in terms which are singularly appropriate in view of the conceptions of our own age. "It became Him, for whom are all things, and through whom are all things, in bringing many sons unto glory, to make the author of their salvation perfect through sufferings." Here is a conception of God's relation to the world which might well be paralleled from the best philosophical thought of the time: "He for whom are all things, and through whom are all things." And it is just because of this vast conception of God's nature that the life and death of Jesus Christ are said to be in harmony with the greatness of God. Think the highest possible thoughts of God, and the sacrifice of the Cross is seen to be most worthy of Him. And the highest thought of all is that God is Love—Love Eternal.

THE LOVE OF GOD IN THE CROSS OF CHRIST

THE RIGHT REV. GEORGE HERBERT MORRISON, D.D.

Minister of Wellington Church, Glasgow, since 1902, *and Moderator of the United Free Church Assembly*, 1926. *He was born in Glasgow*, 1866, *where his father was Principal of the Stow Training College. Formerly minister in Thurso and Dundee and assistant to Dr. Alexander Whyte, Edinburgh, and Sub-Editor of the "New English Dictionary," Oxford. Among his publications are: "The Afterglow of God," "Flood-Tide," "The Footsteps of the Flock," "The Significance of the Cross," "Sunrise," "The Unlighted Lustre," "The Wings of the Morning." He has edited Thomas Boston's "Diary" and Hugh Macdonald's "Rambles round Glasgow," and is a constant contributor to the religious press.*

THE LOVE OF GOD IN THE CROSS OF CHRIST

BY THE RIGHT REV. GEORGE H. MORRISON, D.D.

"*God commendeth His love to us, in that, while we were yet sinners, Christ died for us.*"—Rom. v. 8.

IN our text we are brought face to face with the Cross of Calvary, and we see that Cross standing in a light that glorifies it. That great transaction on Calvary may be viewed in many aspects, but perhaps the aspect in our text is the most sublime of all. Just as the wooden cross itself, that stood upon the hill, was touched with new and ever-varying glories, as the lights and shadows of the setting sun lingered for a moment on its bars, so to the eye of faith new glories fall upon the Crucifixion, under the light of a Sun that never sets. When God sends forth His light, we see the Cross as the master-work of grace. We see the Cross as the gateway into peace. We see the Cross as the type of self-denial. Over and above all that we see the Cross as the one triumphant argument for the love of God. "God commendeth His love toward us, in that, while we were yet sinners, Christ died for us." What is it to commend? It is far more than to recommend. It is to exhibit, to demonstrate, to prove. This then must textually be our theme to-day—the Cross of Calvary viewed as the unanswerable proof of the love of God. First, I shall ask the need that this love should be commended thus. And, secondly, the nature of the love that is thus commended.

I.—Firstly *the need that the love of God should be commended thus*. There are some attributes of God that need no proof. Some features of the Divine character there are, so universally conspicuous as to be self-evidencing. Think, for example, of God's *power*. If we believe in God at all we need no argument to convince us of His power. The mighty forces that engirdle us all cry aloud of that. The chambers of the deep, the chariot of the sun, are stamped with it. The devastating march of winter's storm, and, none the less, the timely calling of all the summer's beauty out of the bare earth—these things, and a thousand other things like these, teach us the power of God. We would not need the cross if all that had to be proved was the Divine omnipotence. Or take the *wisdom* of God. Is any argument needed to assure us, in general, of that? None. "Day unto day uttereth speech of it, and night unto night sheweth forth its glory." Our bodies, so fearfully and so wonderfully made; our senses, linking us so strangely to the world without; our thought, so swift, so incomprehensible; and all the constancy of Nature, and all the harmony of part with part, and all the obedience of the starry worlds, and all the perfections of the wayside weed,—these things, and a multitude of things like these, speak to the thinking mind of the wisdom of the God with whom we have to do. That wisdom needs no formal proof. It is self-evidencing. We would not need the cross if all that had to be proved was the wisdom of God.

Now, brethren, there are not a few who think that the love of God is like His wisdom and His power. Perhaps I should not say they think it, for such a view was never held by a thinking mind. 'Twould be more true if

I said that there are multitudes who vaguely hold that God is Love, and never dream that such a statement calls for some strong argument to prove it. I wish to tell you that that is not the Bible standpoint. I wish to tell you that a shallow optimism like that must ever be rejected by the thinker. The love of God is not self-evident. It is not stamped upon creation like His power. It is not written on the nightly heavens like His wisdom. Nay, on the contrary, if it be a fact, it is a fact against which a thousand other facts are fighting. And if in that love I am to believe, some proof of it, some argument, I must have, strong enough to put these thousand militating facts to flight.

Let me mention one or two of these things that have made it hard for men to believe in the love of God. One is the tremendous struggle for existence that is ceaselessly waged among all living things. Man fights with man, and beast with beast; bird fights with bird, and fish with fish. To the seeing eye the world is all a battlefield, and every living creature in it is in arms, and fighting for its life. The watchword of Nature is not peace, but war. The calmest summer evening, to him who knows old Nature's story, is only calm as the battlefield is calm where multitudes lie dead. Under the outward peace that oftentimes, like a mantle, seems to enwrap the world, by night and day, on sea and land, the bloodiest of wars is being waged. Creature, merciless and venomous, preys upon creature. For right to live, for room to grow, for food to eat, in grim and fearful silence the awful war goes on. Sir, can you wonder that men who have known all that, and nothing more than that, have ceased to believe in the love of God? Can you marvel that he who has no other argument for God's love than what Nature gives him, rejects as mockery the thought of the Divine compassion? Nature groaning and travailing in pain together seems to cry out against the love of God. And in the hearing of these groans, clearer to us to-day than in any past age, only an argument of overwhelming force will convince the heart that God is Love.

Or think again. There are the problems of human pain and sorrow and bereavement. Is it not very hard to reconcile these darker shadows with the light of heavenly love? What is the meaning of the suffering that seemed to fall so causelessly on her you loved? Can God be Love, and never move a finger to ease your little child when he is screaming day and night in fearful agony? Ah, sir, you have had such thoughts as that. Confess them. When in the sudden squall the flower of our fishermen are drowned, when from your arms your dearest joy is torn away, when those who would not harm a living creature are bowed for years under intolerable pain, and when the wicked or the coarse seem to get all they wish, who has not cried, "Can God be Love if He permits all this? How can God say He loves me, and yet deal with me as I could never have the heart to deal with one I loved?"

Brethren, it is such facts as these that make it so hard for many to credit the love of God. It is the experiences of which these are but a sample that call for some unanswerable proof if we are to believe that God is Love. And it is that proof that is afforded us in the crucifixion of Christ Jesus. "God commendeth His love towards us, in that, while we were yet sinners, Christ died for us." The one triumphant argument for the love of God is seen in the Cross of Jesus. The story of Nature may seem to tell against this truth that every heart hungers to believe. And the experiences of life may often seem to fight against it too. But as we read the story of that atoning death, all doubts are overborne. Nothing but love, love wonderful, love matchless, will explain the Cross. When we have gazed in faith upon the Cross of Christ we never can seriously doubt the love of God again. I do not mean that difficulties vanish. I do not say that problems disappear. Much that was dark before remains dark still, but now we bow the head and say we know in part, and with patience wait to be satisfied in the morning. We can be ignorant and dark and even fretful still, but we can never doubt the love of God again. For with overwhelming power God has convinced us of His love, "in that while we were yet sinners, Christ died for us."

Again, observe that this great proof of God's love is a fact and not a word or theory. Love must be proved by deeds, and not by words. The loudest protestations may be empty. No mere profession of the lip will ever satisfy the heart that longs to know another's love. Love's argument is service. Love's commendation lies in sacrifice. The self-forgetful service of the lover wins, as the words of warmest passion never would. And the proof of deeds is needed above all, when by the proof of deeds love seems disproved. If you or I by any act suspect that we are hated, it is not any word, however warm, will ever blot that suspicion out. It is only some deed of love, clear, unmistakable, that will have power to do that. When there are facts fighting against the thought of love, nothing but facts can prove it. See, then, the wisdom of our God. It is the facts of Nature and of life, of history and of experience, that make it so hard to believe His love. He knows it all, and so the proof He offers of His love is a fact too. Facts must be met by facts. And all the dark facts in life God overwhelms by the one proof of the greatest fact in the world's story. Yes, God so loved the world, not that He said or thought, but that He gave. Thanks be to Him for that. I read the loving promises in many of the prophets. I read the passionate language of the Bridegroom in the Song of Songs. And all the time this doubting heart keeps whispering, These are but words! These are but words! Come, thank thy God, my heart, that not in these alone, not in these chiefly has He commended His love to thee. And now I turn to the atoning death of Jesus on the cross. *Here* is no word. *Here* is no empty protestation. Here is a deed tremendous, matchless, irresistible, and every opposing argument is silenced. Looking at Calvary I hear the Lord say, "Come, let us reason together: do I not love thee?" Yes, Lord, I have reasoned with Thee. I have marshalled all my arguments and all my facts, and I am here to confess to-day that by the fact of Calvary Thou hast won.

One other word before I leave this aspect of the case. I want you to observe that this proof is one of perpetual validity. The Bible does not say, God commended; it does not say, God has commended; it uses the perpetual present and says, God commendeth. There are some proofs for the being and attributes of God that serve their purpose, and then pass away. There are arguments that appeal to us in childhood, but lose their power in our maturer years. And there are proofs that may convince *one* generation, and yet be of little use to the next. Not a few evidences, such as that from design, which were very helpful to you, believer of an older school, are wellnigh worthless to your thinking son, imbued with the teaching of this present day. But there is *one* argument that stands unshaken through every age and every generation—it is the triumphant argument of the Cross of Christ. Knowledge may widen, thought may deepen, theories may come and go; yet in the very centre, unshaken and unshakable, stands Calvary, the lasting commendation of the love of God. To all the sorrowing and to all the doubting, to all the bitter and to all the eager, to every youthful heart, noble and generous, to every weary heart burdened and dark, to-day and here, as nineteen hundred years ago to all like hearts in Rome, " God commendeth His love, in that, while we were yet sinners, Christ died for us."

II. *What is the nature of the love that is commended thus?* " God commendeth His own love to us," so the text reads. What is the love, then, that is commended so? And here we must be textual. Wide as the Bible is the subject. All we can hope to find to-day is what the text tells us of this love.

Like life, love is of many kinds. There is a love that ennobles and casts a radiance upon life. There is a love that drags the lover down in the mouth of hell. There is a love that many waters cannot quench. There is a love that is disguised lust. What kind of love, then, is God's love proved to be from His commendation of it?

And first, splendidly visible is this, *it is a love that thought no sacrifice too great.* The surest test of love is sacrifice. We measure love, as we should measure her twin-brother life, " by loss and not by gain, not by the wine drunk, but by the wine poured forth." Look at the mother with her child. She sacrifices ease and sleep, and she would sacrifice life too for her little one, and she thinks nothing of it all, she loves her baby so. Think of the patriot and his country. He counts it joy to drain his dearest veins, he loves his land so well. Recall the scholar at his books. Amusements, intercourses, and sleep, he almost spurns them. His love for learning is so deep he hardly counts them loss. Yes, in the willingness to sacrifice all that is dearest lies the measure of noblest love.

Turn now to Calvary, turn to the Cross, and by the sight of the crucified Redeemer there begin to learn the greatness of God's love. Come, who is this that hangs between two thieves with pierced hands and feet? And who is this whose back is wealed with scars, whose face is foul with spittle? Yes, who is this the passers-by are mocking? See, He is sorrowful even unto death. Hark! He cries, "My God, why hast Thou forsaken Me?" Wonder, O heavens, and be amazed, O earth, this is none other than God's only begotten Son. Did ever mother, did ever patriot, did ever human love in the zeal of love make any sacrifice to be compared with that of God, when He gave His only begotten Son to shame and death, that whosoever believeth in Him should not perish? Ah, sir, measuring the love of God by such a test as this, we touch its height and depth and length and breadth, and then we cry out with Paul, "It passeth knowledge."

Again, I look at the love of God that our text speaks of, and now I see it is a love that never sprang from the sight of anything lovable in us. I suppose in this gathering to-day we have many loveless hearts. There are dead souls within this house of God to-day, all whose affections are slain. And yet I am sure of this, that in all this company there is not one heart but once has loved. Father or mother, son or daughter, husband or wife, once, if not now, you loved them. They were your heart's desire, to them your souls were knit. Well, then, I want you now to recall that love again. I want you to try to trace it to its source. I want you to tell me whence it sprang. Was it the natural outflow of your heart, the welling over of your nature, regardless of the person loved? Or was it not rather some excellence or worth, or beauty, some charms that made an indefinable appeal, that caught and held the tendrils of your heart? Yes, it was that. 'Twas all you saw, and all you knew, and all you conjured, that drew your love out. *You* loved and you loved only, because you found those worthy to be loved. And it is just here that, wide as the poles, God's love stands separated from all the love of men. "God commendeth His love, in that, while we were yet sinners, Christ died for us." God longs to love me into something lovable. But not for anything lovable in me did He love me first. While I was yet a sinner, He loved me. While I hated Him, He loved me. While I was fighting against Him in the rebellious years, He loved me. If we love Him, it is because He first loved us. Such causeless love is wonderful, passing the love of women.

Again, I turn to the love of God our text speaks of, and now I see *it is a love splendid in its righteousness.* Some of the saddest tragedies in human life spring from the moral weakness of the deepest love. Love is the mother of all tenderness, and tenderness shrinks instinctively from what is stern or rigorous. So love, from the excess of her fairest grace, often becomes the minister of ruin. How many a mother, who would have laid her life down for her son, she loved him so, has only helped him down the road to ruin by the immoral weakness of her love. How many a father, to spare his own heart the bitter agony of punishing his child, has let his child grow up unchastened. Such love as that is fatal. Sooner or later it tarnishes the thought of fatherhood in the child's eyes. For in his views of fatherhood the child can find no place now for earnest hatred of the wrong, and passionate devotion to the right; and so the image of fatherhood is robbed of all its ennobling power.

Brethren, I do not hesitate to say that if out of the page of history you wipe the atoning death on Calvary, you carry that tragedy of weakness into the very heavens. Blot out the Cross, and I, a child of heaven, can never be uplifted and inspired by the thought of the Divine Fatherhood again. Yes, I have sinned, and know it. I deserve chastisement and death, I know it. And shall my Father never whisper a word of punishment? and never breathe His horror at my fall? And will He love me, and be kind to me right through it all without a word of warning? I tell you, the moment I could believe *that*, the glory of the Divine Fatherhood is tarnished for me, God's perfect love of goodness and awful hatred of the wrong are dimmed; and all the impulse and enthusiasm these divine passions bring sink out of my life for ever. But when I turn to Calvary, and to that awful death, I see a love as righteous as it is wonderful. Sin must be punished, although the Well-beloved has to die. And the Divine anger at iniquity must be revealed, though the curse fall upon the Son of God. The awful sight of that atoning death assures me of the perfect righteousness of God in the very moment that it assures me of His love. I see the Divine hatred of iniquity; I see the Divine need that sin be punished; I see the Divine sanction of everlasting law in the very glance that commends to me the everlasting love. And now with renewed trust I cast myself again into the arms of that heavenly love. With heart and soul and strength and mind I accept it as it is commended to me upon the Cross. I live rejoicing in the Fatherhood of God. I go to every task and every trial assured of this, that neither height, nor depth, nor life, nor death, nor any other creature, can separate me from the love of God, which is in Christ Jesus my Lord. Amen.

GLORYING IN THE CROSS

THE REV. PRINCIPAL ALFRED E. GARVIE, M.A., D.D.

Principal of Hackney and New College, Hampstead. He is the son of Peter Garvie, linen manufacturer, and of Jane Kedslie Garvie, and was educated at George Watson's College, Edinburgh. He took his M.A. with First-class Honours in Philosophy, Glasgow, in 1889*; his B.A. with First-class Honours in Theology, Oxford, in* 1892*; his B.D., Glasgow, in* 1894*; his M.A., Oxford, in* 1898*; Hon. D.D., Glasgow,* 1903*. He was at Edinburgh University from* 1878 *to* 1879*; then in business in Glasgow from* 1880 *to* 1884*; at Glasgow University from* 1885 *to* 1889*, gaining the Logan Gold Medal as the most distinguished graduate in Arts,* 1889*. He was at Oxford University from* 1889 *to* 1893*; Minister of Macduff Congregational Church from* 1893 *to* 1895*; President of the Congregational Union of Scotland in* 1902*; Professor of the Philosophy of Theism, History of Religions, and Christian Ethics in Hackney and New Colleges, London,* 1903–7*; Principal of New College, Hampstead,* 1907-22*; Chairman of the Congregational Union,* 1920*; and President of the National Free Church Council,* 1924*. His publications include: "Studies in the Inner Life of Jesus," "Studies of Paul and his Gospel," "The Beloved Disciple," "The Christian Preacher," "The Christian Certainty amid the Modern Perplexity," "The Ritschlian Theology," and "The Christian Doctrine of the Godhead."*

GLORYING IN THE CROSS

REV. ALFRED E. GARVIE, D.D.

"*Far be it from me to glory, save in the cross of our Lord Jesus Christ, through which the world hath been crucified unto me, and I unto the world.*"—Gal. vi. 14.

THIS personal confession of Paul, which is interjected in a controversial passage about circumcision, and comes upon us like a bright flash of sunlight out of a dark cloud, contains a historical fact, a theological truth, and an individual experience. It is in the *experience* that the *fact* becomes the *truth*; because for Paul, more than for any other Christian thinker, his personality was the channel of his theology; he could think as he did because he had become what he was. Since he had been crucified and been raised again with Christ experimentally, he could interpret, as no other has done, the Crucifixion and the Resurrection doctrinally. It is in this way, and this way alone, that theology can be made vital; and that in preaching, truth may come through personality. It is for this reason that I have chosen this text for the sermon to be included in this volume, entitled *If I Had only One Sermon to Preach.* While to me for many years the study of the Inner Life of Jesus has been one of the most fruitful means of grace, for me also no less in experience than in doctrine the Cross of Christ is central, as it was for Paul. Nothing as a believer do I desire to know more, and nothing as a preacher do I desire to declare more, than Christ and Christ Crucified.

I

In giving to the Cross this central position, we must not, however, isolate it from what went before and what followed after.

(*a*) Had Jesus not lived, taught, and wrought among men as He did, His death would not, and could not, have had the significance which it had for the community which had been gathered in His earthly ministry. While Paul truly describes the content of the apostolic preaching in the words, "I delivered unto you first of all that which also I received, how that Christ died for our sins according to the Scriptures; and that He was buried; and that He hath been raised on the third day according to the Scriptures" (1 Cor. xv. 3, 4), it must be remembered that the Apostles were companions of Jesus, and had the memory of Him still vivid, as they confronted the problem of His death and sought its solution in the teaching of the Scriptures. We can understand and prize the Cross to-day only as we learn to think, as Jesus has taught us, of God and man, sin and salvation, duty and destiny. It is the person of the Crucified that changes an instrument of torture into a symbol of sacrifice and salvation. It is the glory which streams from His truth and grace which scatters the shadows of the place of execution, Calvary.

(*b*) Even so, yea, still more so, the Crucifixion must not be separated from the Resurrection. Had Christ not been raised from the dead, the faith inspired by the earthly ministry would probably not have survived the shock of His death, and such a death, for the disciples as Jews a death on which fell the curse of God (Gal. iii. 13). For Paul, who knew not the earthly ministry, the

Resurrection alone made the Crucifixion not only tolerable, but supremely significant and valuable. It was only after the Resurrection that the truth concealed in the fact of the Cross was disclosed. Because by the Resurrection He was "instituted Son of God with power, according to the spirit of holiness" (Rom. i. 4), His death was recognised as atoning, propitiatory, and reconciling. We must not then separate the Cross from what led to it, and followed upon it.

(*c*) We must, however, still keep it central. We must not, as many are doing to-day, confine our attention to the teaching and example, the truth and grace of the earthly ministry, and assume that we are receiving the whole divine revelation and human redemption thus. To Jesus Himself the Cross was not only inevitable as a result of His ministry, it was essential as the consummation of His vocation for God among men. Not to mention other indications, one saying, the authenticity of which there is no ground for doubting, is decisive: "The Son of Man came not to be ministered unto, but to minister, and to give His life a ransom for many" (Matt. xx. 28). Such sayings as that about the bridegroom being taken away, and the new wine and the old wineskins, taken together show that at an early stage in His ministry He anticipated that the antagonism between His message and Judaism would have a tragic close. In the later months of His ministry at least He was straitened, until He had been baptised with the baptism and had drunk the cup of suffering. The words at the Last Supper prove that His death meant for Him the sacrifice of the new covenant. The large space given in the Gospels to the story of the Passion as well as the content of the apostolic preaching prove that for the primitive community too the Cross was central. Paul, by the prominence which he gave to the Cross, did not give to the Christian Gospel another character than it had, did not pervert "the truth as it is in Jesus," as some would even rashly dare to say. There have been times in the history of the Church when the Cross lost its commanding position in Christian thought and life. It has been in all ages a stumbling-block to some, and foolishness to others. But again and again has the preaching of the Cross proved the power and the wisdom of God unto salvation. In religious revivals, when Christ has been lifted up, He has drawn men unto Himself. A mysticism which would substitute communion with the living Christ for the experience of the saving grace which comes to men from God in the Cross of Christ, has proved itself equally inadequate to the human need. It is in danger of degenerating into an unethical sentimentalism; for it ignores what for the sinful race in its relation to God is the primary consideration: How can sin be forgiven? How can the sinner be delivered from his bondage, and be reconciled to God?

II

The Cross is so central in history because the truth enshrined in the fact is so essential to theology, the revelation of God which issues in the redemption of man.

(*a*) The description which Paul gives in the text of the Crucified, *our Lord Jesus Christ*, records the ascent of Christian faith. To the personal name Jesus, significant as that was, ascribing salvation to God, was added at Cæsarea Philippi the official title *Messiah* (Christ), as the fulfilment of God's promise of a deliverer was found in Him. After the Resurrection the first Christian creed was, *Jesus Christ is Lord.* The ascription of that title is much more probably due to the Jewish use of it for God instead of the covenant name in the reading of the Scriptures than to any borrowing from pagan cults, as the early current use of the phrase *Maranatha,* "Our Lord cometh" (1 Cor. xvi. 22), proves. In the use of this title the primitive community not only acknowledged Jesus as the authoritative teacher, but called Him its Lord, "because He had brought the sacrifice of His life for it, and because it was convinced that He, raised from the dead, now was sitting at God's right hand." So says Harnack, whom none could charge with theological conservatism; and he adds that it had the authority of Jesus for "placing in the centre this death, the shame of the Cross" (*Das Wesen des Christentums,* pp. 97, 101). In all the types of New Testament teaching, except the Epistle of James (and its brevity may explain the omission), an atoning value and saving significance are ascribed to the death of Christ. In the New Testament the historical fact and theological truth go together.

(*b*) It is impossible in a brief space to expound the doctrine of the Atonement to which, after many years of study and meditation, I have been led; but a few considerations may be offered, which it is hoped may help others to apprehend more fully the significance, and so appreciate more highly the value of the Cross, and thus to enter into clearer understanding and closer fellowship with all believers, to whom the Cross has been what it was to Paul.

Firstly, as a martyrdom, inflicted by human unbelief and hatred and in its circumstances of shame, cruelty, and mockery, the Cross exposes sin in its heinousness and hatefulness. That He who was "holy, harmless, undefiled," "without sin," "going about doing good," loving, tender, gracious, was thus done to death, brings home to the human conscience its guilt, the separation from and opposition to God which sin involves. It is at Calvary that men are constrained to offer to God the acceptable sacrifice of contrite hearts.

Secondly, as a sacrifice, voluntarily offered by Christ in His obedience to God and devotion to man, it makes the appeal of love; and since the Son was revealing the Father to men in His Cross no less than by His teaching, it is the love of God to man which evokes man's faith. The God who can so love is the God who can be fully trusted. There have been theories of the Atonement which have obscured the truth; the Son has been so separated from the Father, that the Son was represented as presenting the sacrifice to the Father, to render Him gracious. But it is God who is in Christ reconciling the world unto Himself. What the Son suffered, the Father suffered in and with Him; and so the sacrifice is God's, the proof of His love.

Thirdly, when men at the Cross apprehend what their sin is, and what God is, their guilt and His love, they realise their need of, and are possessed by the desire for, *forgiveness,* the recovery of the relation to God which sin destroys; that the love of God so suffers from and for man's sin, and is not quenched, conveys the assurance that there is forgiveness with God;

and thus penitence and faith at the Cross receive the forgiveness of sin from God.

Fourthly, while many feel that they need go no farther in their quest for the meaning and worth of the Cross, others there are who are constrained to ask, Why must the forgiveness of sin come from the love of God in this way? Some have answered, Thus and only thus could man be sufficiently impressed with what sin is, and what God is, to repent of sin, and have faith in God's forgiveness. That this is the effect of the Cross, none can doubt; but is that the reason, and the only reason, for the Cross? Many Christian thinkers have answered No, and have sought a reason.

Fifthly, then, while the teaching of Jesus does not carry us farther than that His death was a necessity for the fulfilment of His vocation as Saviour, Paul does not attempt an answer, and men who, like Augustine, Anselm, Luther, may be said to be in the Pauline succession, have tried to reproduce his answer in the language of their own age. Paul in his answer was dealing with Jewish Pharisaism, and we cannot to-day simply repeat his terms. No other Christian doctrine so reflects its intellectual environment as does this; and so each age must have its own theory of the Atonement, and sometimes needs more than one. Each tries to show how the Cross meets what the age feels to be its deepest need. And no theory can claim to have the undivided authority of the Church behind it. In each we may find some suggestion of truth for the enrichment of our own thought.

Lastly, with much diffidence, I submit my own conclusion, reached after much labour of mind, and even distress of soul. There is necessarily in God as holy love a reaction against sin ; He cannot tolerate it, or make compromise with it ; He must condemn it, and execute judgment upon it, as He does in the consequences which in the moral order of the world attach to sin. When as in Christ God offered to the sinful race free and full forgiveness, it was a necessity of His nature as holy love to execute judgment upon sin, not in leaving its consequences to fall on sinners, but in taking them upon Himself in the shame and scorn, sorrow and suffering, death and desolation, that sin inflicted on Christ and God in Him. My conscience at least cannot be satisfied with a forgiveness which does not carry with it a judgment as adequate as the forgiveness is. Such a conclusion cannot be logically demonstrated. As Jesus in Gethsemane recognised the inevitable necessity of His death on His knees in prayer, so only can we.

III

Whatever doubt or difficulty there may be about the reason for the death of Christ, its effect on those who in penitence and faith receive the grace of God, which the sacrifice of the Son and the Father in Him conveys, is manifest.

(*a*) It is the instrument of the creative act of God : old things pass away, all things become new, there is a new creation morally and religiously ; the man is born from above by the Spirit of God, and lives no longer unto the flesh, but unto the Spirit ; he dies unto sin and becomes alive unto God ; he is crucified and raised again with Christ ; he passes out of darkness into God's marvellous light ; he rises out of death in sin into life in God; the world is crucified unto him, and he to the world. In all these ways can the change be described. What needs always to be emphasised is the greatness of the contrast between the life apart from Christ and the life in Christ; the life still unsaved through His sacrifice, and the life His sacrifice is saving.

(*b*) We must not insist on suddenness of change as essential to the reality of the experience. Paul's conversion was sudden for his consciousness, although it was not unprepared in his previous experience. Because of this suddenness, he realised more vividly, and has expressed more forcibly (some who do not understand such an experience might even say violently), the contrast. With others there is a gradual development, in which the contrast is not so vividly realised, and could not with sincerity be as forcibly expressed. What matters is that the change should be experienced, whether it be swiftly or slowly.

(*c*) Without attempting further to describe the change in its many and varied aspects, attention may, in closing, be called to that particular aspect which the words of Paul indicate: by the Cross the world was crucified unto him, and he unto the world. What Paul meant is more fully indicated in the passage in Philippians (iii. 1–11) in which he shows what he had once prized as a Jew and Pharisee, and had counted as dung that he might gain Christ. That world was not only dead, but dead through the execution of a judgment of condemnation upon it; it had ceased to have any value or attraction for him. He was dead to it, and on him too as an apostate judgment had been executed by his unbelieving fellow-countrymen; he had their hatred and scorn, and was enduring persecution at their hands. The circumstances of the Christian of to-day are very different from Paul's; but is there not, and if not, should there not be, some counterpart of this experience?

(*d*) Many Christians are so conformed to the world around them, that they show little evidence of being transformed by the renewing of their mind. Much as the Christian leaven may have pervaded the whole lump of human society in lands nominally Christian, yet the change is not so complete that there is never any occasion for the world to be crucified to the Christian, or for him to be crucified to the world. The customs, standards, and institutions around the Christian to-day have not yet been so transformed by the Spirit of God that he can afford to be conformed to them, if he desires to realise the Christian character. For instance, there is on the part of many Christian business men an acquiescence in methods which from a truly Christian standpoint must be condemned. Ruthless competition, the deliberate forcing of rivals out of the trade, the driving of workers at greater speed than their bodily strength allows—these are not Christian. The success of many men in business is an evidence of their failure as Christians. There are Christian women who conform to fashion in the costliness of their dress and the luxury of their homes to such a degree that it is difficult to believe that they can be successfully cultivating the Christ-like life. In politics men will do for party or country what they would hesitate to do in self-interest, what they certainly could not justify to a sensitive conscience.

(*e*) The hope of human society being Christianised does not lie with the Christians who thus conform to the world around them; it lies with those who have been so transformed by the change which the Cross of Christ has effected in them, that they are indeed crucified unto the world, and the world unto them. Much which the world values the Christian cannot prize; what he values the world must despise. From the Cross of Christ there comes the challenge to the safe, easy, and comfortable Christianity of to-day, accepted and approved even in many Churches, to realise the antagonism, and necessary antagonism, of the world as it now is to all Christ is and is doing.

(*f*) Such nonconformity means sacrifice, it may be outward, it certainly is inward. Still, very many things that the world counts gain must be reckoned loss for the excellency of the knowledge of Christ Jesus as Lord. Ambitions must be subordinated to aspirations. Human companionships must be given up for the closer communion with Christ. Hardship must take the place of comfort, and toil of ease, if the Cross is taken up, and Christ is followed. Accordingly the Cross must be no less central in practice than in experience, in morality than in religion. And so intimately related and mutually dependent is the one upon the other that the grace of the Cross cannot be apprehended unless the duty of the Cross is accepted, and the duty of the Cross cannot be done unless the grace of the Cross is gained; the free giving and the free receiving of the Cross as Divine grace and human duty go together. It was the love of Christ, as displayed in His Cross, which constrained Paul not to reckon himself as his own; and it is only as the Cross of Christ means to us and does for us what it meant and did for Paul that we, even as he was, will be crucified unto the world, and the world unto us. To glory in the Cross of Christ without this crucifixion in ourselves is a vain boast ; only when this result follows from that cause can it become a personal confession, which God will approve, and bless with the increase of His grace to the glory of His Name.

A VISION OF GOD

THE BISHOP OF WINCHESTER (THE RIGHT REV. FRANK THEODORE WOODS, D.D.)

Ex-officio Prelate of the Order of the Garter; Hon. D.D. (*Camb.* 1916, *Edin. Univ.* 1922). *Son of the Rev. Frank Woods and of Alice Fry, daughter of Joseph Fry, who was the youngest son of Elizabeth Fry, the well-known philanthropist. He was educated at Marlborough College, and Trinity College, Cambridge, and ordained in* 1897. *After holding curacies in South London and in Manchester, he became successively Vicar and Rural Dean of Bishop Auckland, and subsequently of Bradford. Bishop of Peterborough,* 1916–24; *he was translated to Winchester,* 1924. *Select Preacher at Cambridge,* 1917 *and* 1920, *and at Oxford,* 1918–19. *He accompanied the Archbishop of Canterbury to the General Assemblies of the Church of England and of the United Free Churches of Scotland to bring to their notice the Lambeth Appeal for Reunion,* 1921. *Publications: "Lambeth and Reunion" (joint author with the Bishops of Hereford and Zanzibar), "Interpreters of God," "The Great Fellowship," "Great Tasks and Inspirations," "The Revised Prayer Book."*

A VISION OF GOD

BY THE BISHOP OF WINCHESTER

"*Sir, we want to see Jesus.*"—St. John xii. 21.
"*He that hath seen Me hath seen the Father.*"—St. John xiv. 9.

A VISION of God—that is above all else the need of the world and, more particularly, of our generation. If I had only one more sermon to preach I would concentrate all my emphasis on this. We need it, we in England, and in these days. The very controversies of the moment have exposed the fundamental interest of our people in religion and at the same time the very inadequate conceptions of God which are rife among us. It is important, no doubt, that we should be aware of our animal ancestry, if only to keep us sensibly humble. It is much more important that we should think rightly of the precious gifts in the Holy Communion. But behind all there is the idea of God, for on its idea of God, in the long run, depends the behaviour of any generation, its neglect of or its capacity for righteousness and truth.

All that we most need to-day, that strong sense of duty, that purity in social life, that readiness to share instead of to grab—all these qualities come ultimately from a sense of God. According to the presence or absence of that sense the barometer of a nation's moral fibre rises or falls as certainly as the glass in your hall reflects the anti-cyclone or the disturbance from the Atlantic; only its movement is slower and less perceptible. That that barometer is none too high is sufficiently obvious. In great tracts of life it is the stark fact that God is not known. This is in striking contrast to earlier days. Men's supreme concern was to know God. He might be found in the cloud or in the thunder; in the totem or in the temple; but at all costs He must be discovered, and the entire regulation of life, whether for the tribe or the individual, was framed in accordance with His will so far as it could be ascertained.

The same was true in our own land and not so long ago. It is not too much to say that right thought of God and the right worship of God was the supreme interest of the sixteenth century and certainly of the seventeenth. For the Royalist and his Prayer Book, for the Puritan and his Bible, this was an interest of the first magnitude, and they would as soon have thought of dispensing with their ideas of God as of dispensing with their daily food. To us in the twentieth century such a state of affairs seems dim and distant. There may be things—luxuries, perchance—which we cannot dispense with, but we can dispense with God—not perhaps deliberately and openly, but in those assumptions and actions which speak so much louder than words. Why is this? Why is the sense of God so dim? Why is He so little known? He used to be in the foreground. Why is He now relegated to the background? I will suggest one or two answers. For one thing, there is a vague notion in many minds that science has so laid bare the inner workings of the universe and so explained its processes that the Creator has, so to speak, been crowded out. But it does not follow that, because you find the railway system mapped out to the minutest detail in the time-table, there is no general manager and no engine-driver. On the contrary, the more orderly as well as intricate are the ways of nature the more wonderful must be the mind which directs it and the energy which propels it. This is true of that amazing procession through the ages which we commonly call Evolution. It is equally true of that consummate adaptation of means to ends which abounds in every part of God's creation and most of all in man himself. In the words of a wise observer, "the ingenuity which can fashion an eagle out of the stuff of its reptilian forbears, or can accomplish the miracle of hearing by transforming gill-slits into Eustachian tubes, reveals the economy of a god." We may add—assuming the truth of what was said at the British Association meeting of 1927—that much more marvellous is the ingenuity which can put such stuff into an animal that it will develop into a man, and the skill which can pilot the creature across the mysterious gulf between matter and mind and between flesh and spirit. So far from science tending to oust God, its real effect, for those who have eyes to see, is to enthrone Him and to exhibit His methods of working in a way and on a scale which before the nineteenth century was practically unknown.

Another reason for the dimness of our sense of God lies in the extraordinary extent of man's command of nature. If it cannot be said that the winds and the sea obey him, it is true that he increasingly compels them to serve his purposes, and the same is true of the fire and the lightning. You have only to think of the mechanical inventions connected with steam, electricity, and air, during the century since 1827, to realise that civilisation, at least on its mechanical side, has progressed a hundred times faster during that period than in the thousand years preceding. When my grandfather went back to school after the holidays from London to Darlington it meant a journey involving two nights on the top of a coach. Now, a boy, if he does not slide back in his father's limousine, sits for an hour or so in a comfortable compartment. The element of danger hardly exists. The ingenuity of man has conquered every difficulty. So far from its being an adventure to cross a river, the car or the train is across it before the passengers are aware that there is a river. So completely is man in command that any other power seems superfluous. The phrases of the Litany—those at least which speak of danger and anxiety and need—seem to belong to a different world to the one where, seated in your comfortable armchair, you listen to the orchestral concert, or with the telephone to your lips speak to your friend a hundred miles off. In such a world as this where does God come in?

Nor is this all. The very multiplicity of interests so occupies the attention of the ordinary man that he has neither time nor inclination to look beyond them. So varied, so attractive, so absorbing are the things temporal, that the things eternal, as we say, hardly get a look in. Whereas a hundred years ago the average man scarcely knew what was going on outside his own village, in this year of grace his interests are literally world-wide. Every evening he listens to the news which has been collected from every quarter of the globe. Apart from this, what with his work, his games, his hobbies, his amusement, there is so little time left for more serious things. Not that his recreations are to be regretted.

They are, or should be, part of the joy of life. Part, not the whole. And there can be no satisfying joy for the man who leaves his soul untended, and who, when faced with the graver questions of life, gives a shrug of the shoulders and looks the other way.

But the Church itself—that is, we ourselves—is to blame for the lack of the sense of God. We have in great measure ceased to give the impression that God is real. This is partly due to our "unhappy divisions." But it must be remembered that they are due in part to the depth of feeling which is aroused in men where questions of faith and worship are concerned. To put the matter crudely; devout men demand a Church where the highest view of God prevails, and their failure to secure this has been before now a prime motive of schism. Further, we live in an age when this unfortunate exhibition of disunion is fast being counteracted by the world-wide movement towards reunion whose momentum is daily increasing. It is sufficient to mention the words "Lausanne" and "Stockholm" to bring this vividly to mind.

But it is not the spectacle of disunion which hinders the Church from making God real; it is the feebleness of her moral witness. There are so comparatively few lives in which obviously God makes all the difference. Mercifully there are some. Most of us have known one or two. It may have been a father or a mother or a friend whose goodness and unselfishness were redolent of God. That young man I came across the other day who had refused a business career of brilliant promise in order to devote himself to the ministry; the girl who, though a great favourite in society, insisted that her Sunday-school class and her work in the parish must always have the first place in her list of engagements. Such people—and they are not too uncommon even in these days—give the impression that God matters. They help to counteract the other impression that numbers of church people when it comes to the crux do not really believe that God is to be reckoned with. Often, for instance, when it is a question of dealing with money or property, or with the provisions of a will, the religion which is supposed to occupy a prominent place in the hall seems to disappear through the back door. In naked questions of gain or loss God does not count.

The fact is that, to some extent at least, our religion has been secularised. And the reason partly is that people have misunderstood its bearing on the great moral enterprises of our day such as the League of Nations, or industrial fellowship, or social purity. These enterprises are splendid and Christian, but they are not Christianity. Christianity is contact with God in Christ and the eternal life which results therefrom. It is because in Christ we see God that we begin to understand what qualities God most values and what tasks God wants done. We must not mistake the house for its foundations, or the tree for its roots. The only really permanent incentive for these and other enterprises is a vivid sense of God. No vague humanitarian enthusiasm is sufficient. The well-known lines of Burns are full of warmth and kindliness, but they are not religion:

> The social, friendly honest man,
> Whate'er he be,
> 'Tis he fulfils great nature's plan,
> And none but he.

Great nature's plan is not so easily ascertained. Nature can be red in tooth and claw. But God's plan is ascertainable. Christ was God in terms of human life, and Christ was sociable and friendly. But He was so much more. His sociableness brought Him to the Cross, for He was more concerned to redeem the world than to pander to the prejudices of His day. His friendliness was wonderful, but only a dozen men or so were prepared to avail themselves of it to the full. In other words, He insisted on living solely by God's standard, and the message He proclaimed was concerned with a world far greater than this one and with a life in which our earthly existence is only an episode. He lifted men out of their ordinary world and gave them an eternal life, and the result was a love for their fellows and a longing for their salvation—body, mind, and spirit—which was and is the mainspring of all personal and social betterment. Here we come upon the familiar paradox which is always worth pondering, namely, that "it is other-worldliness that alone can transform the world." Look at the men and women, in the nineteenth century for instance, and in our own land, who did most for the betterment of their fellows. Think, for example, of Wilberforce and Shaftesbury, of Elizabeth Fry and General Booth, to say nothing of scientists like Pasteur and Lister, or divines like Kingsley and Westcott. What is the outstanding feature of their characters? Precisely this, that they lived in humble contact with God. To them God was more real than anyone or anything else. They believed in an eternal life, and in consequence they were all out for the uplift of their fellows in this one. We have foolishly imagined that by leaving out God and the fear of God we could more easily get on with the work of reforming the world. Whereas literally our only chance of progress is to restore the sense of God; the valuation which sees life in the vista of eternity. The plant can no more dispense with the sun, nor the cathedral with its foundations. To realise God, in the New Testament sense, is to put one's own life in order and to be in a position to help others to do likewise. For love is the soul of progress, and God is Love.

But how to realise God? That is the question. One thing is certain: it must be God's own action. The entire history recorded in the Bible is the story of God's actions in making it possible for men to realise Him. God is always first in the field. Whether it was by prophets or by punishments—the ministry of an Isaiah or the experiences of a captivity—the aim was the same: to make God real to men. This was the purpose of Christ's coming, and if God in His mercy thought fit to go to that immeasurable length of love and sacrifice, can we suppose that He is any less anxious now than He was then to make Himself known? But now, as then, the first step rests with Him. It must be, it will be, a movement of His Spirit. We are powerless to produce it. But we can do our part.

For one thing we can think. That seems obvious, so obvious as to be hardly worth saying. But how many of us devote even five minutes in the day to deliberately thinking about God, with or without the Bible open before us? Many people no more think about God with any care or definiteness than they think about the bread they eat or the chair they sit on. Yet considering what we know about Him and what we owe to Him, is it possible to conceive a more interesting subject for thought? I admit that this deliberate attempt to be quiet—to meditate, in the full sense of that word—is not congenial to our modern mentality, nor easy in the racket and bustle in which most people have to live their lives. Yet the whole psychology of "suggestion" emphasises the necessity of selecting and ordering the thoughts on which we dwell, and a high authority [1] has informed us that "the soul is dyed the colour of its leisure thoughts." But that colour is primarily determined by the thoughts which are not casual, but deliberate. Here indeed the country-dweller has an obvious advantage. In the country, more easily than the town, men can realise God. They are close to the mysteries of nature. They have more opportunities for reflection. How many Scottish thinkers, for instance, learned their art at the plough or with the sheep! Free from the manifold distractions of the town, a man can watch the wonders of earth and sky, of bird and beast. With that book on the one hand and his Bible on the other he can begin to find out God. Our country life is worth restoring for this reason, even if there were no other, that we shall be providing conditions in which it is more possible to be quiet, to think, to pray. For it is sacramental.

> I had no God but these,
> The sacerdotal Trees,
> And they uplifted me,
> "*I hung upon a tree.*"
> The sun and moon I saw,
> And reverential awe
> Subdued me day and night,
> "*I am the Perfect Light.*"

[1] The Dean of St. Paul's.

Within a lifeless Stone—
All other gods unknown
I sought Divinity,
"*The Corner-stone am I.*"

For sacrificial feast
I slaughtered man and beast,
Red recompense to gain,
"*So I, a Lamb, was slain.*"

Yea; such my hungering grace,
That whereso'er my face
Is hidden, none may grope
Beyond eternal hope.[1]

Through nature, through men, through things, God manifests Himself. To us is given the chance of understanding that on a stupendous scale the material is the vehicle of the spiritual. Gone for ever is the old idea that matter is essentially evil and spirit is essentially good. Matter can be the channel of the highest. Spirit may be the incentive of the lowest. But in God's intention the world of sense is the interpreter of the world of spirit. In the lines of Francis Thompson:

Lo, God's two worlds immense,
Of spirit and of sense
Wed
In this narrow bed;

Yea, and the midge's hymn
Answers the seraphim
Athwart
Thy body's court!

---

[1] John Bannister Tabb, *An Anthology of Jesus,* edited by Sir James Marchant, p. 258.

And we of all people should be able to appreciate this. Whole regiments of physical things, from the electric current to the ether waves, have now been commandeered by the spiritual; and what with the wireless and the rays, we walk in a world of ever-increasing marvel. The spiritual is always breaking into the material and, like a flash of lightning on a dark night, lighting up the whole sky. Every day we are confronted with men and women either in the past or the present who, defying what might be called the urge of safety first, hear an imperative command from the higher world, and obey it. It may be a Francis going forth to persecution and poverty; or an Irvine and a Mallory going strong for the summit; or a medical martyr in the cause of science; or a priest working in an East-end slum; or a missionary spending his life in the smells of some Eastern bazaar or holding his classes in the pygmy forest. There is nothing natural in these adventures. Nothing to be gained. No money to be made. Nothing is owing here to man's "gorilla descent." It is supernatural. It is the urge of a greater world. It is the spirit capturing the flesh. It is the spiritual breaking into the material. It is the temporal yielding place to the eternal. And it does so in ways that we can all understand. To borrow a phrase from the schools, the vision of God is graded. It comes to men on the step to which they have attained and to which they are accustomed. To Isaiah in the Temple; to Simon Peter in the fishing-boat; to St. Joan in her homely kitchen and in the village church; to Charles Kingsley as he went about his parish. And there, at the very centre of history, is the Vision of which this is supremely true. God condescended. God accommodated Himself. God stepped down till He reached our level. And we behold Jesus. There at the meeting-point of ancient and modern, of the old world and the new, "the Word was made flesh, and dwelt among us, and we beheld His glory . . ."

Just because through the modern study of the Gospels we have grasped, as possibly no generation since the first has been able to grasp, the reality of our Lord's humanity, we have been able to grasp with a deeper insight the reality of His deity. For though He is so human, the more you measure Him by human standards the more unaccountable He is. Natural through and through—let Nicodemus and the Woman of Samaria and Martha and Mary testify to that, to say nothing of Peter and John and the others. Yet supernatural, as they all discovered. Perfectly at home in both worlds. But proving at every turn that this world with its human interests and situations, its common ways and its ordinary furniture, can be and is intended to be the framework for the exhibition of that other world. One of our profoundest thinkers and mystics has called attention to the fact that in our generation the two main lines of spiritual advance seem to be the rediscovery of the historical Jesus and the worship of the ever-present Christ in the Holy Communion. There is great significance in this. We want to get down—if I may use the vulgar phrase—to the brass tacks of history, and see face to face the humanness of God in common life. On the other hand, we want to grasp afresh the reality of the supernatural, and discover anew that whatever may be said of the circle of the natural and the human, our one hope and joy lie in the fact that God breaks into it; uses it to His purpose; makes it the channel of His self-giving to man. For obviously this relationship of the material and the spiritual reaches its climax —apart from the Incarnation itself—in those great moments when the Lord makes Himself known in the Breaking of the Bread. In all the ways of which I have spoken He makes Himself known; in the stars and in the flowers; in the heroism of the man; in the selflessness of the mother; in the purity of the little child. But here is the focus and climax of it all. Simple as bread and wine can be; yet mysterious, for here the Eternal breaks into the material; God stoops down to man. And this has been the experience of the Church throughout the ages. The witness of millions is behind the familiar words:

> Thou spread'st a table in my sight,
> Thy unction grace bestoweth;
> And oh! what transport of delight
> From Thy pure chalice floweth.

Ever since He said of those so common things, "This is My Body; This is My Blood of the New Testament," men in every century have found that there, simply yet wonderfully, is His Presence; that eating that bread and drinking that cup they were partakers of His life.

But the manifestation of the spiritual through the material, whether in stars or flowers or men, is not dependent on the capacity of people to perceive it. It is *there*. So it was in the supreme manifestation. Very few perceived it. "He came unto His own, but His own received Him not." So it is still. Yet multitudes in the Church have felt, however dimly and imperfectly, that ineffable Presence, and have joined—

perchance this very day—in the words in which we seek to express our obeisance:

> Thee we adore, O hidden Saviour, Thee,
> Who in Thy Sacrament dost deign to be;
> Both flesh and spirit in Thy Presence fail,
> Yet here Thy Presence we devoutly hail.

Not that the Presence is limited by its sacramental expression. But, in Miss Underhill's beautiful words, "It is the taper in the window which tells us that the Master of the house is at home."

And this brings us to the conclusion of the whole matter. The Vision is there. In the universe; in nature; in those lives and characters in which we catch a glimpse of the supernatural; supremely in Jesus our Lord; and in that high moment when He makes Himself known to us in the Breaking of the Bread. And the Vision is within the reach of each and all of us if with a humble, lowly, and obedient heart we draw near. Watch for it—in your prayers—as you lift your heart to God before you go out to work. Get that New Testament open again and study it. Gaze on Jesus as He moves among men from the manger to the Cross and on to the open grave. And, seeing the Vision, see all else in the light of it. The men and women in their multitudes for whom He died. The homes which He could make happy and holy. The service which in Church or Nation, in home or parish, which, for love of Him, you might render, the people you might help. For to see God is to love men.

Be on the look-out for God in your own life. To do this is not to be a visionary. Precisely the opposite. We move every hour in the midst of what is utterly practical, completely common, thoroughly pedestrian. Yet it is there that the curtain is drawn back and God comes into the open. As you sit at your desk, as you walk down the street, as you mend the children's clothes, as you work in the office, as when you kneel in the church or at your bedside, you can touch God. And that brings healing and energy and power. For God is unveiling Himself to all who will look. He is speaking to all who will attend. He is loving all who would be loved.

> My God, how wonderful Thou art,
> Thy majesty how bright,
> How beautiful Thy mercy-seat,
> In depths of burning light !
>
> How wonderful, how beautiful,
> The sight of Thee must be,
> Thine endless wisdom, boundless power,
> And awful purity !
>
> Yet I may love Thee too, O Lord,
> Almighty as Thou art,
> For Thou hast stooped to ask of me
> The love of my poor heart.

Then give it. And give it now.

THE SUPREME QUEST

THE REV. REGINALD JOHN CAMPBELL, D.D.

Born in London in 1867, he is the son and grandson of Nonconformist ministers: Ulster Protestants of Scottish extraction. He was educated at University College, Nottingham, and Christ Church, Oxford, where he graduated in Honours in the School of Modern History and Political Science. In 1895 he entered the Congregational Ministry at Union Chapel, Brighton; and from 1903 to 1915 he was in charge of the City Temple, London, in succession to Dr. Joseph Parker. Ordained in 1916 into the Ministry of the Church of England, he was attached to Birmingham Cathedral, and became Honorary Chaplain to the Bishop of that Diocese. In 1917 he returned to London as Vicar of Christ Church, Westminster. In 1919 he obtained the degree of D.D. from Oxford University. Dr. Campbell is now Incumbent of Holy Trinity, Brighton—the church made famous by the ministry of the Rev. F. W. Robertson. Amongst the volumes which he has published are: "The New Theology," "Christianity and the Social Order," "The Ladder of Christ," "Thursday Mornings at the City Temple," "A Spiritual Pilgrimage," "Words of Comfort," "Problems of Life," "Life of Christ."

THE SUPREME QUEST

BY THE REV. R. J. CAMPBELL, D.D.

"*Fight the good fight of faith, lay hold on eternal life, whereunto thou art also called.*"—1 Tim. vi. 12.

IT is impossible to apprehend the true bearing of this exhortation without reading in connection therewith the whole chapter of which it forms part. The recipient of this apostolic letter, a young man who has been placed in a position of some spiritual authority, is being bidden to avoid all worldly seductions and concentrate his desires upon the one great thing which constitutes his vocation. Thus: "But thou, O man of God, flee these things—that is, worldly things—and follow after righteousness, godliness, faith, love, patience, meekness. Fight the good fight of faith, lay hold on eternal life, whereunto thou art also called."

Then follows a solemn adjuration to be faithful to this commission until the second coming of Christ took place, whenever that might be. "I give thee charge in the sight of God, who quickeneth all things . . . that thou keep this commandment without spot, unrebukeable, until the appearing of our Lord Jesus Christ; which in His times He shall shew, who is the blessed and only Potentate, the King of kings, and Lord of lords; who only hath immortality, dwelling in the light which no man can approach unto; whom no man hath seen, nor can see; to whom be honour and power everlasting. Amen."

It has been conjectured that this fine ringing succession of appellations—Blessed and only Potentate, King of kings, and Lord of lords, the sole possessor of immortality, dwelling in light unapproachable, whom mortal eye has never beheld—formed part of an early Christian hymn, sung in the regular assemblies of the Church for worship. As a description of the Supreme Being it may have been derived from contemporary Greek sources; Platonists could and did use this kind of language; it was common enough among the Gnostics. Does it here refer to God the Father only or to God as revealed in Christ? There is good reason to believe that it includes both. It is God in Christ who is the supreme object of the soul's quest, but remains ever hidden and remote except as self-communicated to the heart that seeks Him in humility, faith, and love.

There is therefore an intentional importance in what is here so earnestly urged upon a youthful servant of Christ. He is to maintain a warfare for his faith, to lay firm hold upon eternal life and let all lesser things go, to put away from himself everything that would hinder him from attaining to the one all-inclusive good that man can know in this or any other world.

We do no violence to the meaning of the counsel so impressively given in these terms if we say that the appearing or manifestation of Christ here alluded to as the Christian's dearest hope can be mystically as well as historically construed. There is plentiful justification for this statement, not only in the Pauline letters, but in the Johannine writings. That the primitive Church lived in the intense expectation of the visible return of Christ in glory is of course obvious to any reader of the New Testament; but it is equally true that that consummation was felt to be anticipated in the experience of those who had laid hold on eternal life. There is a revelation of Christ in the sanctified soul, a parousia, an unveiling of the divine majesty in the inmost shrine of our being, which is in itself salvation, or rather the realisation thereof, and is the most precious possession that any of us can either know or desire as long as we dwell in this our earthly tabernacle.

Permit me an aside here for a moment or two. The word "mysticism" is one of the most misused of our time. Many people claim to be mystics or talk about mysticism who know little of what the great Christian mystics of the past either were or taught. They confuse mysticism with agreeable religious emotion or even with psychic abnormalities such as visions, auditions, and ecstasies. This kind of dilettantism—occasionally verging upon eroticism—is as far as possible removed from the mysticism of, say, St. Catharine of Genoa or St. John of the Cross. We should not feel at all attracted to-day by the terrible self-inflicted austerities of these types, and they in their turn would reject with scorn any suggestion that supernatural visions and voices had necessarily anything to do with their main quest. The great mystics were great sufferers. What they sought was union with God, and they were convinced that this was only obtainable by being crucified to self and the world. It does not follow that we ought to imitate their methods; on the contrary, such unnatural macerations are to be deprecated; but we do need to be as wholehearted in our pursuit of the one thing needful. There is a mystical element in all Christian life, namely, immediate apprehension of the presence and the love of God. It matters little whether we use the name or not; this is an essential of all higher experience, and without this it is hard to see how spirituality, properly so-called, could exist.

One further point before we pass on to consider the main message of the text. What is here asserted of God, and the very terms employed in so doing, are quite definitely applied to Christ elsewhere in the New Testament. In the Apocalypse, by a daring conjunction of metaphors, we are told that one who is the lamb slain from before the foundation of the world is also King of kings and Lord of lords. In the Fourth Gospel we are told that He is the Light of the world; and in a fine Pauline phrase, that God, who commanded the light to shine out of darkness, has shined in our hearts, to give the light of the knowledge of the glory of God in the face of Jesus Christ. The Fourth Gospel again, in its opening chapter, says of the apostolic Church, "We beheld His glory, glory as of the only begotten of the Father." And it is the same hand that, in the first of epistles which bear the name of St. John, says almost in the very words of my text "No man hath seen God at any time; if we love one another, God dwelleth in us, and His love is perfected in us." Nor should it be overlooked that this precise expression, "No man hath seen God at any time," has a prominent place in the prologue to the Fourth Gospel, where it completes itself in the explicit affirmation, "The only begotten Son, who is in the bosom of the Father, He hath declared Him."

The message of my text, then, is just this. The one fundamental reality behind all that we know about ourselves and the world in which we live is the being of God. It is a fact that has far more to do with us than any other fact that enters into our experience. But what do we positively know about God? At first hand nothing. "No man hath seen God at any time." He is at once the most unescapable fact in our lives and the most inscrutable. Yet if we could only know God as He is, if the veil were only taken away from before our eyes, or, to put the truth more accurately, if only our eyes could be opened to behold the invisible and eternal, we should have found that which would for ever make an end of all that has power to hurt us and hold us in bondage. All that oppresses and hinders us in our quest for satisfaction, all that makes us burdened, anxious, afraid, or sad at heart, all our delusions and misgivings, would disappear like shadows dancing on a cloud. If we could uncover, if only for a moment, that underlying, all-pervading, all-comprehending Divine life without which nothing is or could be, we should be utterly at rest about the problem of living in all its vast and various modes and meanings. These would have no more dominion over us; the darkness would be swallowed up in the light of God's own presence.

This is what sanctified souls, the adepts of the spiritual life, have always told us with united voice. But there are those among the voices of to-day, as in every previous age, who tell us something very different about the ultimate mystery of existence; and if they be right, it were surely better that we should know the truth, however unwelcome. We are all standing, as it were, before a drawn curtain, the curtain that veils from us the great secret, the knowledge of which would explain everything, including ourselves. What is on the other side of that curtain? I do not mean on the other side of death; I mean on the other side, the inner side, of all the knowledge we at present possess of what we are and whence we came.

There are those, of course, and they are not few, who do not want to know what is on the other side. They either shrink from it, or are indifferent to it, or take for granted that everything desirable is on this side, not on that. These are what we may rightly call materialists—not in theory, but in practice. Materialism as a theory is dead; no one really holds it now; but materialism in practice is very much alive. In fact, I should say that there never was a time in the history of our civilisation when men were so absorbed in the contemplation of the things of sense or so satisfied therewith, to the virtual exclusion of all interest in the things of the spirit. They do not want to look on the other side of the curtain or to know anything about what is there.

Let us be sure that my use of a figure of speech is not being misunderstood. I repeat that I am not speaking of the screen that interposes between this life and the next, between the world that now is and that wherein we shall find ourselves after death. That is not what is in my mind at all. I am speaking of the veil of mystery that hides from us the real meaning of the life that now is; by what is on the other side of that veil I mean the all-pervading, ever-present, yet hidden Divine life and power without which nothing that we know could exist for a moment. I mean that fundamental fact or force or substance, or whatever you like to call it, which no scientific instrument will ever touch, which neither telescope nor microscope will ever reveal, but from whose operation none of us can get away for a single instant, that in which we live and move and have our being, which comes far nearer to us than any outward things, and is the source of every breath we draw and of our very ability to know ourselves. It is this, I say, which so many people are content to ignore at the present day while engaged in the strenuous and engrossing pursuit of ends which hardly matter a jot.

On the other hand, there are some serious minds which insist that there is nothing on the other side of the curtain. Bertrand Russell is a very able thinker, though a pessimistic one, and he and all his school declare emphatically that the quest in which we are here and now engaged is sheer waste of time, that religion is merely a pathetic delusion, a soporific, a drug wherewith we try to give ourselves pleasant dreams. A representative of this school said to me not long ago, " You really do not want the truth; what you want is to persuade yourself that behind the veil of sense there is concealed a heart that feels for the miseries of mankind and a power that will set all things right; what you and your fellow-Christians want is not truth, but an anodyne."

This is a charge frequently brought against adherents of the Christian faith, but it is quite untrue. No ordinary mind can rest for long in what it suspects to be a lie; we are under compulsion to face the truth, however dark it be. And if the gospel of Bertrand Russell be the truth—and not only his, but that of other teachers who see less clearly than he the implications of unfaith—it is indeed a melancholy resting-place for our souls. Russell and those who think with him would not admit that they were materialists, nor are they in the strict sense of the term ; they do not blink facts nor affect an optimism for which they see no justification in the constitution of things. But there are other teachers, such as H. G. Wells, who try to delude themselves and us by a continual whooping about the greatness and the glory, the wonder and the triumph, the splendour and success that still await humanity on this planet. This is a creed that accords well with the mechanisation of the globe that is so rapidly going on. The achievements of science are indeed stupendous and we do well to admire them ; but if we seek to make of them a substitute for the fulfilment of our spiritual cravings, we are woefully self-deceived. In the last resort the individual matters more than society, paradoxical though it sound to say so ; and the individual has little to gain from all this speeding up of life which is going on. Leave God out of the reckoning, and the future of the individual is but little brighter than it ever was. Here is a power which all men know, an inner urge which all men feel, compelling them on occasion to superhuman effort in obedience to high spiritual vision, but a power that knows nothing of their toils and sorrows, cares nothing for their moral grandeurs, and leaves them to perish hopelessly at the last. Do not let us hoodwink ourselves : this is a gospel of despair ; it plucks the very soul out of everything great and noble that has ever been attempted by human will or accomplished by human faith. And there are many more among the voices of the time, some charged with moral passion, others with none ; some with a call to betterment, others with neither idealism nor hope in their accents ; who bid us forbear to entertain illusions as to what lies on the other side of that curtain towards which in our best moments, and in all our deepest and truest experience of life, we turn a wistful gaze.

There is much, very much, in life which appears to tell in favour of this camouflaged pessimism, for that is what it is even at the best. Life is a fight in any case ; but what are we fighting for ? and is the fight worth while ? Now and then the pessimism is undisguised pathos. A distinguished soldier, a man of fine religious nature, as is true of so many of the world's best fighters, put forth a book of confessions years ago, wherein he told how his own thoughts were brought to a focus on this point. Walking along a country road he was run down by an automobile and seriously injured. For months he lay in hospital, enduring the most terrible pain while slowly struggling back to life, and here is what he says about it : " I have described my sufferings at length and in detail, not because there was anything unusual in them, but because they are so very common, because there is so much worse suffering in the world, and because, reflecting on all this suffering, I could not help asking myself whether the usual view of things could possibly be correct—that we were under the care and guardianship of a kind and almighty Being who was ever watching over us to protect us from all evil." What is there, he asked, behind the veil of mystery that shadows all mortal existence ?

The answer to this challenge is my text, which is in itself a challenge, as this noble-minded soldier ultimately realised. There is an indefeasible experience which all men may have, but at a price, an experience to be set over against what I have just been citing. Once get possession of it, and the most urgent problems of life are solved. It is not an easy experience to arrive at; it would not be worth much if it were. One of the greatest mistakes that anyone could make would be to imagine that the Gospel of Jesus Christ is one easy of acceptance. It is far from being that, as His own recorded words make sufficiently clear. It demands everything we have to give—ourselves, our earthly prospects, our love of ease and reputation, and even our dearest attachments, whatever they may be, if any of these happen to come between us and His service. As Dean Inge says, God never intended to make faith easy; the highest values in life have to be fought for and won. The love of God in Jesus Christ is the greatest thing in the world; it is the one good that includes all other good that can be imagined or conceived. If you set your heart on that and pursue it with all your might, turning neither to the right hand nor to the left, you will not fail to find it. You will be doing what the Apostle counsels his youthful helper to do in the chapter before us. He is to follow after the one great thing, the one thing needful, and turn away from all that would hinder him in his quest or come between him and his objective. "But thou, O man of God, flee these things—the things of this world . . . fight the good fight of faith—or *the* faith; the faith as it is in Jesus—lay hold on eternal life."

Dr. Rufus Jones reminds us that we all have to live by two sets of values, primary and secondary—those which are rightly termed eternal, and those which are temporal. The latter include all the ordinary, everyday ends of our activity—the winning of food and shelter, the maintenance of health and home, the service of those we love and of the community to which we belong. But in all these and apart from them there is a greater and more abiding good to be sought, a good which will still be ours in undiminished fullness—nay, in greater and more glorious measure—when all things earthly have passed away. To be possessed of this is to be possessed of that knowledge of God in Christ which is in itself eternal life.

But, understand, there can be no compromise. The supreme quest must ever be kept in view and everything else subordinated to it, and that means a hard fight with the old Adam. It will mean that you are being made over again, as it were, in the likeness of your Lord. It will mean, for instance, as old Thomas à Kempis puts it, that you will strive as earnestly to escape being honoured and praised and admired by men as others do the opposite. It will mean that you centre your thoughts and aims as intensely on spiritual reality as others do on secular success. And then by and by the miracle will happen. The curtain will lift. You will become as sure of God and of the fire of His love that burns up all the corruption of our nature as other men are sure of money or pleasure or gratified ambition. And you will never want to exchange the one for the other. When the love of God lays hold of us, when we become conformed to the likeness of Christ, we are at the very heart of the mystery of existence. It is limitless life, love, power, and bliss all in one. This it is which was from the beginning, is now, and ever shall be, world without end. "And we all, with unveiled face beholding as in a glass the glory of the Lord, are changed into the same image from glory to glory, even as by the Spirit of the Lord."

THE TRUSTWORTHINESS OF GOD

AGNES MAUDE ROYDEN

Miss Royden is the youngest daughter of the late Sir Thomas Royden, 1st Bart., of Frankby Hall, Birkenhead. She was educated at Cheltenham Ladies' College and Lady Margaret Hall, Oxford. She worked for three years at the Victoria Women's Settlement, Liverpool, and then in the country parish of Luffenham. Miss Royden joined the National Union of Women's Suffrage Societies and became a member of the Executive Committee, from which she resigned in 1914. *She also edited "The Common Cause." During the years* 1917–20 *she was Assistant Preacher at the City Temple. She was the founder, with Dr. Percy Dearmer, of the Fellowship Services at Kensington in* 1920, *which have now been transferred to the Guildhouse, Eccleston Square. Amongst her publications are: "Women and the Sovereign State," "The Hour and the Church," "Sex and Common-sense," "Political Christianity," "Prayer as a Force," "Friendship of God," "I Believe in God."*

THE TRUSTWORTHINESS OF GOD

BY AGNES MAUDE ROYDEN

"*The Father of lights, with whom is no variableness, neither shadow cast by turning.*"—Jas. i. 17.

THE saints have believed in the trustworthiness of God, "with whom is no variableness, neither shadow cast by turning"; the world has never believed it. Only now and then have men caught a glimpse of the great truth that God is changeless and that His changelessness is our peace.

For the most part we have both believed and hoped that God might be capricious. We know of no man so good that we should wish him never in any particular to change, and, making God in our own image, we hope that, good though He be, we shall persuade Him—as a sincere and eloquent pleader might persuade one of us—to be a little better, to change His mind. We wish He might be at times more merciful, more full of compassion to us when we think we need it most; or more relentless and less pitiful to our enemies, who, we fear, may be besieging His throne of grace with their impious and unwarrantable petitions at the very hour of our own prayers.

Long ago, nevertheless, the caprices of God were seen to be a source of trouble rather than of consolation. It seemed that in a moment of well-justified wrath He had decided to drown us all and have done with it. In fact, He lost patience—a very human thing to do!—but in the end He was sorry and "repented Him of the evil," again very like a human being. So a handful of men and women were saved and the trouble began all over again. Then comes man's first glimpse of the great truth that it is not from a capricious but from a constant God that men may look for assurance and mercy. "The Lord said in his heart, I will not again curse the ground any more for man's sake, . . . neither will I again smite any more every thing living, as I have done. While the earth remaineth, seedtime and harvest, and cold and heat, and summer and winter, and day and night shall not cease. . . . And God spake unto Noah, and to his sons with him, saying, And I, behold, I establish my covenant with you, and with your seed after you. . . . This is the token of the covenant which I make between me and you and every living creature that is with you, for perpetual generations: I do set my bow in the cloud, and it shall be for a token of a covenant between me and the earth. . . . And the bow shall be in the cloud; and I will look upon it, that I may remember the everlasting covenant between God and every living creature of all flesh that is upon the earth." [1]

This is the beginning of a nobler idea of the Divine. The caprice of God had nearly destroyed life: His promise henceforward to be trustworthy was recognised as a condition which made life possible, for without seedtime and harvest in regular succession men cannot support life. When the inspired writer added that the beauty of the rainbow was the pledge of this constancy, he had already perceived that Law was Love, for beauty is always the expression of love.

The idea, however, that Law is Love and the unalterable laws of God absolutely necessary to our develop-

[1] Passages from Gen. viii. and ix.

ment and freedom is one which we still find it very difficult to hold. We accept, and glibly repeat, such texts as the one I have taken for this sermon. We say that in God " there is no variableness, neither shadow cast by turning "; that He is " the same yesterday, to-day, and for ever "; that for the guidance of the universe He has made " laws which never shall be broken."[1] We still, however, hope that, notwithstanding, our prayers, sacrifices, or ceremonies may induce God to change His unchanging mind and suspend His immutable laws. Too often we pray not so much that we may understand and fulfil His laws as that He may relent and make them a little less austere. We even contrast the love of God as revealed to us in Christ with the relentlessness of nature, and ask ourselves anxiously whether it is possible to reconcile the two. Nature, we think, is law, and all the universe is governed by law so unchanging and unchangeable as (at least) to save us the trouble of trying to argue with, suspend, or change it. Christ, we think, revealed to us a very different God—One who is love, and who will certainly yield to our prayers if we pray earnestly and faithfully enough.

Such ideas as these should already be impossible to us, I think. They would have been so, if theologians had not, by a tragic error, fought against the revelations of natural science. They thought that a world so subject to law as that revealed by the scientists of the last century must be a world in which human freedom was impossible. They thought that law meant slavery and was the denial of free-will. They even lost their faith in God sometimes and left the unlearned and the

[1] Hymn paraphrased from Ps. cxlviii.

orthodox more frightened still by reason of the terrible fate which had overtaken the students of science.

It is difficult now to measure the depth of such fear, for the nightmare has passed away and the truth has made us free.

We know now that a constant and lawful universe is one in which we can not only be free, but be masters. We know this, not by arguing about it, but by seeing it happen. We have watched the conquest by scientists of such terrifying forces as water, steam, gas, and electricity. We see men plunging under the sea and returning in safety. We see them soar up into the air and watch them without a tremor. We see great areas of the earth's surface reclaimed from the sea, or from disease and famine, and made into healthy, wealth-producing places. We are so accustomed to these marvels that we marvel no more. We learn with interest but without astonishment that our voices can be broadcast round the earth or that someone has flown the Atlantic. We are moved to admiration by the courage of the flier, but we are no longer astounded that he should succeed. We have learned to expect success —if not to-day, to-morrow; if not to-morrow, next year.

We should, then, find it easy to believe both that God is unchanging and that His unchangingness is not terrible or relentless, but merciful. We should by now be finding it difficult to believe anything else. How could God, who is One, be changeless in a material universe and capricious elsewhere? Why do we still try by prayer to change the mind of God, and, when we fail, speak of "resigning ourselves to His inscrutable will"? Christ taught us not to be "resigned" to the will of God, but actively to carry it out. Even in the Old Testament we are called upon to understand God—"Come now, let us reason together, said the Lord God"[1]; to stand upon our feet—"Son of man, stand upon thy feet, and I will speak to thee."[2] How strange that in the twentieth century people should still be found to sing "Thy will be done" as a sort of refrain or chorus to verses containing a list of frightful misfortunes, each of which, it is implied, must be "endured" as coming from the hand of God; when the words used ("Thy will be done") were uttered by our Lord Himself as a promise that where the will of God is done, there the kingdom of God is established, so as to make a heaven on earth.[3]

Christ appeals to His disciples continually to understand His teaching—not to be resigned to His inscrutable will. He told His hearers that those who failed to live by His teaching were foolish—not that they were wicked.[4]

His teaching here is in striking contrast to that, for example, of the author of the third chapter of the Book of Genesis, though both are teaching the same truth. If, said the latter, you eat of the fruit of that tree, God will kill you, for it is His tree, and He forbids you to touch it. Or (as he might have said in other words), "If you build on sand, God will smash your house, for sand belongs to Him and He has warned you off it." In other words, the teaching of Christ implies a constant God; the teaching of the other writer an arbitrary one.

The laws of God are not, to Christ, like the laws of men which may be broken: they are like the laws of

[1] Isa. i. 18.
[2] Ezek. ii. 1.
[3] Matt. vi. 10.
[4] Matt. vii. 26.

nature (also God's laws) which cannot be broken. We cannot break God's laws, but we can break ourselves against them or go from strength to strength in their power. And the reason is this: that God, like nature, is unchanging and unchangeable. Because He is so, we can learn to use His powers. "His service is perfect freedom." In Him there is no uncertainty or caprice. Having once grasped this truth, we must, and clearly we will, give up trying to change His mind by prayers or sacrifices. We shall instead try to understand His mind and make it ours. We shall in our prayers unite ourselves with His purpose. In doing so we shall find ourselves working mighty works, and our Lord's amazing promise will come true for us: "He that believeth on Me, the works that I do shall he do also; and greater works than these shall he do."[1]

This amazing promise (which Christians have rarely believed) is no promise of exceptional powers over natural or spiritual law. There is nothing here of the conjurer or of the conjuring trick; no claim to suspend the laws of nature or of God; no insistence on exceptional powers, either for Himself or for His disciples. "The works that I do shall ye do also," using the same power in obedience to the same laws.

This is the attitude of the scientist, who never claims for himself the power either to break or to evade the laws of nature. His assurance to us is in such words as our Lord Himself used, that "he that believeth on us, the works that we do shall he do also"—and ultimately, without doubt, greater works than any scientist who yet has lived has done.

But "law" and "laws" are cold words to living,

[1] John xiv. 12.

struggling, suffering men. We may know that there is law and may try to understand and obey it; yet we fail. It is too hard for us. Where is the law written down that we may learn it and obey it? The Ten Commandments? Surely this is not all! They do not satisfy us, neither do they give us that power over life and over ourselves that we so long for and so worship in Christ. These codes of law, lofty though they be, solve nothing for us. They are dead things. They do not help in their own fulfilment; they only condemn our failure. "All these have I obeyed from my youth up: what lack I yet?"[1]

We lack Christ. The law is nothing to us until it is lived. The Ten Commandments solve no mystery of life, pain, or perplexity for us. Christ superseded them with a law which is love and of which love is the only fulfilment. He lived this law of Love among men, bore suffering as ourselves; and we beheld His glory, the glory as of the only begotten Son of the Father, full of grace and truth.[2]

Laws are not enough for us. We want a life to show them in action and in power. We want to see the One who proclaims the law live in perfect obedience to that law without once seeking to break, evade, or suspend it; and we want to see that, in fact, what He said was true—that such obedience is power, such service perfect freedom.

We want Christ.

While the scientist, still confessing his ignorance, gropes after knowledge and, even in groping, finds his hands laid on the levers moving the universe, his mind adjusted to astounding powers, Christ, in the perfection

[1] Matt. xix. 20. [2] John i. 14.

of His knowledge of a higher and a deeper world, moves armed with power and seeming to work miracles among men.

In one sense there are no miracles; there is no breaking of any law, spiritual or natural. In another sense all life is miraculous; we cannot explain the miracle of life itself. We do not know by what miracle love creates love, nor why hatred destroys. In our own lives, and supremely in the life of Christ, we see—we see to demonstration—that it is so.

If a code of rules had been enough, the Ten Commandments would have sufficed; or if not, then the Ten Commandments explained and fulfilled by the Sermon on the Mount. But a code of rules is *not* enough; even the Sermon on the Mount is not enough. A book can tell us something, but not all. Our Lord therefore lived the law for us, and we see that the law is love. It is noticeable that, so little are words sufficient, if we take Christ's actual words, so far as we know them, and lay them side by side, we find that they often contradict each other. "He that is not with us is against us." "He that is not against us is on our side." Which of these is true? "If any man strike thee on the right cheek, turn to him the other also"; but Christ, when struck on the cheek, remonstrated. "Resist not evil," said He who drove the money-changers from the temple. "Judge not," said the unsparing Judge of the Pharisee and the Scribe. "Peace I leave with you; My peace I give unto you: not as the world giveth, give I unto you." . . . "I come not to bring peace, but a sword."

I think our Lord used the language of paradox and uttered Himself in seeming contradictions because He had to: the things He spoke of were too great for our human language. Christ therefore chose to speak in parable and paradox, knowing that we could never obey a law into which we had not entered in the spirit. In order to understand His law, we must mentally and spiritually labour and sweat. We must learn all we can. We must try to enter into Christ's mind. We must seek the meaning behind His words. How could we do this unless we had a life to illustrate the law? How could He trust us to do it if He Himself had written a book? We should have sat down to read the book and get the law by rote! Now we must both read the books His followers wrote and try to understand the spirit of the Man of whom they were written.

It is difficult to learn from a book of rules how a game should be played or an art acquired; so difficult as to be in fact impossible. So it is one thing to know the law of one's country by heart and quite another to be a patriot. We must indeed learn the rules of the game and listen to the great teaching of the master of our chosen art, but we must also watch him play the game or paint the picture. At the least we must see the picture he painted and try to understand how he applied the counsel he gives to us.

Christ, the great Master of life, moved among men as a conqueror. For myself, I believe that He both healed the sick and raised the dead, calmed the storm and rose on Easter Sunday from the grave; but even for those to whom these are mere fairy-tales there remains the supreme miracle of the life of Christ—the change He made in the hearts of men. In a short life of from thirty to thirty-three or four years, this man of lowly birth, without wealth or influence or powerful backing, so changed the history of the world that we date now every event in its history by its distance in time from His coming. " Before—or after—Christ "—such is the dating of all our records. Christ cut the history of the world in half.

And this He did by no use of force or of wealth; neither the fear of armies nor of magic entered into His appeal. He achieved all by love. The precepts of conduct which, in cold words, sound either fantastic or unmanly, He made real and glorious by His own life. He gave to all who asked and He lacked nothing. He met hatred with love and unbelief with an authority which owed nothing to astonishing feats of magic. He never defended Himself, and we see in Him the bravest of the brave. He took the sword out of the hand of His friend and went like a lamb to the slaughter, and we cry in admiration, " Behold the Man ! "

It is useless to argue that Christ's laws can never be carried out, for He carried them out Himself; to protest that they are inconsistent with themselves, for the utter consistency of Christ silences the protest on our lips; useless to complain that they are unmanly, for no man ever was so gloriously and perfectly a Man.

It is only when we see how patience and courtesy and " non-resistance " look in Jesus Christ that we realise how empty is the mere commandment—how powerless without the living Example. This only deepens for us our knowledge and belief in Christ's assurance that God is Love. To turn the other cheek ! To endure all things, to believe all things ! How pitiful it sounds in the ears of the noble, sagacious, and courageous pagan ! But when he sees all these in Christ, can he despise them any more ? They may seem too high for him—they cannot seem too low for him. They may be set aside as too hard—they can never again be utterly despised.

And so it happens that nearly all men have loved Jesus, though not all worship Him. If God is Love, it is more important to love than to believe, for it is only love which has power to create us in its own image. God is Love.

Here, again, life is based on universal, immutable law. Not Eloi alone, four thousand and four years before Christ, created man in his own image, but Love (which is God) always and everywhere does this. We become, by irresistible compelling, like what we love. This is true of the least as of the greatest. So, loving Christ, we learn to live as He lived and to obey the laws which He obeyed. Law is no longer a dead and empty thing, serving only to condemn us for our failure to keep it: it is a living power, enabling us to obey.

Thus Christ was the Word of God, creative and creating in God's image according to His words. "And the Word was made flesh, and dwelt among us, (and we beheld His glory, the glory as of the only begotten Son of the Father,) full of grace and truth."

GOD'S PURPOSE FOR MAN

THE REV. WILLIAM EDWIN ORCHARD, D.D.

Minister of the King's Weigh House Church, Duke Street, W., since 1914. Dr. Orchard received private tuition, and later went to Westminster College, Cambridge. He was ordained at Enfield in 1904. In the following year he became B.D., and D.D in 1909. His publications include: "Evolution of Old Testament Religion," "Modern Theories of Sin," "Problems and Perplexities," "The Temple: a Book of Prayers," "The Outlook for Religion," "Divine Service: Order of Service for Public Worship," "The Devotional Companion," and "Foundations of Faith."

GOD'S PURPOSE FOR MAN

BY THE REV. W. E. ORCHARD, D.D.

"*I shrank not from declaring unto you the whole counsel of God.*"—Acts xx. 27.

THERE are apparently very few people to-day who have any conception of the vast, rich, majestic structure of Christian theology; for few have the time or capacity to read a sound and full exposition of the Faith, and the demand for sermons extending to not more than twenty minutes gives no time to declare the whole counsel of God, and only produces trivialities. To open a theological treatise, such as the mediæval Schoolmen or the early Reformers could produce, is to be impressed by its very size, comprehensiveness, and logicality, and it might at least be felt that there was something to be said for a religion which could produce such consistent thought and construct so vast a system. And this impression is deepened when it is recognised that the motive of this system is not the love of mere dialectic or speculation, but is an endeavour to show how the purpose of God in the salvation of the human race gives the only adequate explanation for existence, runs like an immanent purpose through all things, involves all life, and yet awaits the acceptance of the individual soul. Whatever may be thought about the truth of Christian theology, in no other system are the vastness of the universe and the processes of history so brought to bear upon individual decision as the purpose for which the whole exists: it is not only extensive in its range, it concentrates all the forces of existence to extract from the soul a decision which shall put that vastness in its possession.

Seeing, however, that some souls will come under the sound of the Gospel but once; that for everyone there will be some occasion critical for its acceptance; and by every soul it will once be heard for the last time, there is necessity, sometimes at least, for making the whole system visible, and always for enough to press the point of personal decision. There used to be a society which demanded of its evangelists that on every proclamation of the Gospel they had to mention the seven points which were believed to be essential. Although these were perhaps stated somewhat narrowly, and the effect of such a direction was bound to become somewhat mechanical, there was sound sense in the demand. To-day, however, every doctrine has been questioned, so that in attempting to evade difficulties we fall into truism, vagueness, and platitudes. But when we remember that all modern inquiry is now focusing itself on one personal and insistent question: Why do I exist? if Christianity can answer that question, there ought to be a point of contact here between its whole system and the most pressing and personal inquiry of the modern mind.

The great difficulty, of course, is not only that of compression, without losing the force of its appeal and reducing the pressure of its vitality, but an enormous amount of time has to be spent in refuting counter-arguments and removing objections. Apart from this being a lengthy task and of its raising as many questions as it answers, sometimes, at any rate, it would be a better answer to every possible objection to try to state the system as a whole. Sometimes in private interviews with those inquiring about the truth, or seeking the answer to intellectual difficulties, when it becomes apparent that no real progress is being made, time is short, and it is likely that the inquirer, disappointed, will be seen no more, I have felt moved to say: "I know that I have not persuaded you, and I have given you no clear and convincing argument on the points that have been raised, but before you go, without stopping to defend, explain, or justify, I am going to state to you what I believe to be absolutely true about God's purpose for you, which then I must leave to you to accept or reject; I must do this in discharge of my commission and conviction, in the hope that it may remain in your memory and be considered when your need makes you more open to understand and accept it." It is something like that I want to do now.

THE ETERNAL PURPOSE OF GOD HAS BEEN REVEALED

1. This was to create a society of souls that should form the body of Christ.

(*a*) This purpose was always in the mind of God.

It was not an idea that came into His mind at a certain time; the Word of God, the Second Person of the Blessed Trinity, the Eternal Son of the Eternal Father, was and is that idea, He being the perfect image of God, the personification of all God's thoughts; so that, in Him from all eternity, all that has ever come to be was already present, not only in thought, but with the purpose of realisation, the explanation and potency of all actual and future existence. To bring into existence a society of souls is to give to those ideas a life of their own, in which, bonded together through personal fellowship in union with Christ, these souls should reflect the glory of God in such a way that they shall rejoice in the light and love of God with that same joy which is the very life of the Godhead. It is a movement, therefore, to externalise the thoughts of God in a multitude of personal experiences. So great is the bliss of God, and so great is the love of God, that He would have others enjoy His existence and share His nature.

(*b*) The realisation of this eternal purpose in others demands that immense and mighty output of energy known as creation.

It includes, first, the forming of the ultimate basis which we call time and space; it means bringing into existence that wonderful store of energy which contains within itself the possibilities of material construction, the higher combinations of organic life, and the supreme possibilities of mind, with its consummation in myriads of personal, conscious souls, welded into one organic society, at once their ground and their end. The vastness of time and space, which we are gradually discovering to be immensely greater than once was thought, the linking up of the whole material, organic, mental, and spiritual life in one co-ordinated and reciprocating scheme, only enhances the value that must be set upon the conscious, mental life, to which alone this scheme becomes visible, and by which alone it can be valued. The bringing of such souls into conscious, corporate, and satisfying communion with God is the only worthy end of existence, and alone explains the expenditure of such enormous power, the patience of such sustained processes, the long historical development necessary to enable the mind to understand the value of existence, to become aware of its ultimate purpose, and to realise that purpose in personal union with God and our fellows.

(*c*) In this scheme man stands distinct, unique, and consummate.

Greater than the material world, on which he depends for a foothold, the organic world, on which he depends for food, and the animal world, which has contributed towards his physical frame, man is nevertheless created as an imperfect being, because he is created capable of further development. Here he is differentiated from another type of being, namely, the angelic order. Although created perfect, spiritual beings of pure, unhindered intelligence, capable of beholding the glory of God, at which they are thrilled to inexhaustible and ceaseless praise, and although higher than man in power, the angels are destined to be outstripped by him in nature, and indeed are only created in order to serve man by their material and spiritual ministrations. Man is created a little lower than the angels, unable to behold God as He is, but only indirectly, or through some condescending theophany; but he is possessed of a craving to see the face of God, to be like Him, and to enter into personal and spiritual union with Him. It is this end, higher than that which any angel can attain or even desire, which necessitated man being created imperfect and unfinished; for ultimate, personal union with God could only be possible with man's own decision. Man is therefore made in a condition in which his destiny can be slowly disclosed to him; slowly it must be, lest its ultimate height should seem for him too high, and he should at once refuse it as impossible. While he is given a soul that desires God and can never be satisfied with anything else, he is given powers of decision concerning himself which are absolute, and can be made irrevocable when he has reached a sufficient knowledge to know all the consequences of such a decision. He is given a body, not to clog this process, but in order to temper the revelation as he can receive it; his physical senses providing a veil against the exceeding brightness of the glory of God, which at last he is to behold and will be invited to share. Further, his body, by its constitution, prevents him from descending to a lower stage, and so becoming unaware of God's purpose; the cravings of the body being themselves unsatisfiable, and so bringing into relief the higher satisfactions of the soul as the only final satisfactions even for the body. The animals, whose evolution may have contributed to his physical constitution, remain to remind him of his own difference from them, and the disaster that would overtake him if, possessing these cravings, he were to sink to an animal level; the beasts warning him against the dangers of falling, the angels setting a standard beyond which he himself may rise.

2. This purpose of creation is not allowed to be hindered by sin.

(*a*) The creation of these perfect angelic beings led to a fall.

It is, in the nature of the case, impossible that a being could be perfect without being free, and even for the angelic order it was necessary that they should be given a choice, even if it had to be swift, instantaneous, and irreparable, as with their perfect endowment of intelligence it could be. Soon after the angels were created, the supreme among them, the Archangel Lucifer, rebelled against his condition, probably because he was not equal to God; and perhaps because man was to be made higher than himself. With those of the angelic host who decided with him, he was immediately banished from the presence of God, which had become to him intolerable; the decision, both of the angels who maintained their first estate and of those who fell from it, being by its nature final; the sight of God's glory together with the gift of freedom entailing such a decision and fixing it for ever. This was the first tragedy of creation. But the purpose of God was not to be deterred by this tragedy; His justice allowed to the angels the freedom of their decision, but it was His wisdom that, despite this, His purpose should not be abandoned.

(*b*) Man being created with freedom and yet with an imperfect nature made a further fall possible.

Not only is the possibility of a wrong decision inherent in that very gift of freedom which is necessary if man is to accept a destiny that by its very character demands his free choice; but God foresaw what man's decision would actually be. Man's decision was liable to be perverted by temptation on the part of the fallen angels, who out of envy and malice might attempt to deflect man from his destiny by making specious promises that it could be reached independently of the purpose of God; thus at once firing his heart with an ambition to be divine, and instigating it to rebel against the Divine means for achieving it, so reproducing their own fall: the fall of man being partly a refusal to rise to God's purpose, and partly an attempt to snatch at only half of it.

Divine foreknowledge does not necessitate human sin; neither does man's being created imperfect, nor the possession of a body which he shares with the animals compel him to sin; and never is man merely deceived by the specious promises of diabolical temptation. Why man should have sinned, and why, although man now inherits a tendency to sin, he goes on sinning, we shall never explain; for sin is essentially an irrational act, and therefore inexplicable. For man's sin is not simply disobedience to his Creator's purpose, since in his present condition his Creator's will for him is often unknown; but it is always a sin against his own reason: either by denying the verdict of reason which points to the Divine origin of the universe, the immortality of his soul, and the freedom of his choice; or by allowing bodily cravings to rebel against reason and demand unreasonable satisfaction, when they themselves became a danger to the body's constitution.

But whatever be the ultimate mystery of sin and the guilt it lays upon us all, not only that it was possible, but that it would certainly take place, God foresaw; but His Eternal Purpose was not to be inhibited by that possibility or that actuality: first, because His purposes are not to be hindered by anything outside Himself, which would be the abandonment of His Godhead; and secondly, because the resources of Godhead are such that He is not only able to overcome sin and reverse the Fall, but actually to use it to make His purposes known and to hasten their fulfilment.

(*c*) Although sin has brought such suffering and misery to the universe, and has had such far-reaching effects, this does not deter the Divine Wisdom from completing the Divine purpose.

Sin has involved the whole creation ; this not only through the mental blindness and weakened will of man, but in the purpose to which man is now directing his life according to his own will. To make nature serve him was the original intention ; man also has been given almost unlimited powers of improving nature, and of making new combinations of natural forces that otherwise would never have come into existence ; but at the same time he can pervert these powers to selfishness and destruction. The very working of the external world may have been rendered less perfect by the conflict between the good and the evil angels, so that all kinds of natural catastrophes happen which may have formed no part of the original plan. The animal world also shares in the Fall ; partly through the influence of the evil spirits, and partly through man's bad example, their instincts are perverted to cruelty by preying upon one another, and development now takes monstrous forms and produces unbalanced multiplication. Worse than this is the increasing temptation to sin provided by sinful example, by man's bringing into existence a diseased and perverted posterity, and above all, the cruelty, both mental and physical, which he is constantly perpetrating upon his fellows ; until it is possible for man to look back upon the history of the world and see in it such deluge of blood and tears that he goes on to make this a count against the goodness of the Creator, curses God for His own gift of freedom, and wishes that he had never existed, thus bringing upon himself a further hopelessness and the depression of despair. The terrible story is not yet ended, the awful conflict between good and evil is not yet decided nor, so far as this earth is concerned, is it predictable ;

nevertheless, not only was all this foreseen by God, but the Eternal purpose is still maintained, because God is able to use all that has happened as the very means by which that purpose can be attained. Although the Fall need not have happened, the fact that it was not only possible, but foreseen, was woven into His Eternal plan, the very Fall being used of God to drive man beyond the state of his original innocence, in which he had communion with God, and making him desire something further still, namely, that which the Eternal Son has always had with the Eternal Father, a union of perfect love.

3. To attain the Divine purpose the Incarnation of the Son of God was undertaken in order to reveal man's predestined image.

(*a*) Not only is the nature of God revealed beyond all possibility of doubt by the appearance in our world of the Son, who is the image of the Father; but the Son also reveals the image in which we were made, namely the original purpose stamped upon us, which was to become also ours through our free choice, thus making us like God.

The Incarnation of the Son of God opens more to man than was originally possible to him as created; for not only can man now see God in the Incarnate Son, and enjoy that communion to which Christ freely invites all men, even the most sinful, but He teaches men how they may become like God. This is, however, what man does not altogether want; therefore the appearance of the Son of God in our midst has a most extraordinary result, precipitates a great conflict, and forces sin to disclose its real nature. The original desire for God, implanted in the mind of man, burns afresh as man now beholds the nature of God in the person of the Incarnate Son, and his desire for God is immensely increased. At the same time all the forces of evil, natural, human, and diabolic, gather together to resist this desire, with the result that the Son of God is not only rejected, but His death is determined upon, carried out with every species of insult and cruelty, with the motive not only of ending His earthly career and of covering the Divine appeal with shame, but of destroying the Divine Love, thus making a complete end of God. This comes to an issue not only as an historic fact in the Crucifixion of Jesus Christ, which has branded human history with its supreme and unforgettable crime, but the Crucifixion only bodied forth the interior motive and ultimate aim of sin, namely, the resistance of the Divine voice, the rejection of the Divine destiny, and the attempt at destroying the action of God's Spirit within us.

(*b*) The consequences of this consummate sin are, however, turned to the fulfilment of God's purpose.

All man's sins have wakened in him a certain consciousness of guilt and a certain reaction of remorse; but this final sin of crucifying the Son of God produces in his own nature an immense reaction, as murder of any kind always does, and opens the way to repentance. But by accepting the Cross, and by His Resurrection, Christ shows man that He absolutely forgives this chiefest of sins, and therefore all man's lesser sins; but He also shows that Love cannot be destroyed. The result is that when anyone recognises and admits that he has really crucified the Son of God, and goes on to recognise that the Son of God was willing to be crucified for him, by this accepted sacrifice the nature of God, which is love, stands revealed, and man's own nature is so drawn to that, that he can hardly forbear loving such love. If this love, which springs up quite naturally, is yielded to, it is bound to carry the soul farther, and at length unite it to Jesus Christ in such a close, personal and spiritual way that it makes the soul a member of Christ's Body, and by that means introduces that soul into a corporate communion which makes possible its entrance into the interior life of Deity, bestowing upon it all the love, all the glory, and all the joy which Christ eternally has with the Father.

(*c*) This redemption flows out to embrace all humanity. There is enough love and power manifested in the Cross to persuade the greatest sinner of forgiveness, and, if he yields to its power, to lead him to entire sanctification and final union with God. As each soul comes to know this is the meaning of existence, he inevitably makes it known to others, either by the proclamation of the Gospel or the influence of his example. But this action upon others only gives point to a redeeming purpose that has been in operation ever since sin entered the world. What we call the historical evolution of man, the development of human society, the increase of knowledge, beauty, and goodness, have always been due to a redeeming purpose ministered interiorly in every soul, and immanently through all society, by the incessant working of the Holy Spirit. And why the sin of man has never had the results upon individual souls, or upon society, which it really ought to have had, is because it has been constantly countered by this redemptive process. The whole of the moral and secular progress which, despite sin, has also marked the history of man, is due entirely to the action of that redeeming love which broke forth into more compelling revelation and more effective power in the Cross of Christ; and that redeeming love will always go on, whatever man does. So that souls who in this world refuse the forgiveness and grace offered in Christ nevertheless partake of the benefits of a world that has been redeemed and a civilisation which is in process of Christianisation. And even though their decision may be one of rejection, at length as final as that of the fallen angels whose company they may elect to be their own, the redemption wrought by Christ will make an enormous difference even to their condition. Deprived of the vision of God, and the end of their destiny perverted, they will nevertheless not reach the conditions they would have created for themselves if it had not been for the Sacrifice made on their behalf by Christ.

This Purpose has to be Accepted by the Individual Soul

1. This individual choice is essential to the realisation of the purpose.

(*a*) The beatific vision of God can be granted to no soul without its consent.

A sufficient vision of God will be granted to all men with or without their consent; but to remain regarding that vision, or to hide away from it, must be their decision. Communion with God must first be offered to man apart from his choice, but each soul must choose whether that communion shall be consummated in complete and eternal union. No union between the soul and God can be possible without a high degree of consciousness having been reached, and that demands, at least, the full knowledge of what God offers to us, a choice that is absolutely free, and an understanding of what is entailed.

Nothing will be done to destroy our freedom of choice. All the pressure of God's presence upon the soul, the presentation of His truth to the mind, the offer of salvation, the disclosing of His glory, all must stop short of coercion, because coercion would destroy the very purpose that is proposed. At the same time there must come a time when man is able to use his freedom with such perfect knowledge that he can make a choice that shall be irrevocable. Therefore all God's revelation of Himself to man works up, first, through a craving for God implanted in the heart, then the bringing of the knowledge of God to bear upon his mind, and the pressing upon his soul the attraction of sanctity, until if man assents at every step and so far, at length God discloses Himself in His glory, and in that instant the spirit of man is presented with the final choice, and will then gladly surrender the power of further choice, and be thus united to his Creator in eternal love.

(*b*) The power to make this choice marks man's greatness.

The very fact that God has given this freedom, that God will never force it, and yet that man can use his freedom to fix his purpose for ever, is the measure of the immense greatness bestowed upon man and purposed for him. If we shrink from the responsibility that this choice puts upon us, the rejection of responsibility would only take us back to something lower ; if sometimes we wish that the grace of God were invincible, again that would surrender the very greatness that He has in mind for us ; the highest gift He could bestow on us is the freedom to determine our own destiny. And just as the goal of all physical evolution is the development of conscious personality, so all spiritual evolution is designed to confront every conscious personality with the infinite Person of God, that the great decision may be freely, fully, and finally made: either to rise to God's glory or reject His purposes for us. The ascent can only be made by God's grace, the descent will be entirely man's responsibility. That grace will never be withheld from those who desire to ascend; and that freedom will never be withheld from those who determine to descend.

2. The purpose is racial, the acceptance must be individual.

(*a*) The purpose of God is the salvation not only of every individual soul, but of humanity as a whole: that is, not only separate personalities, but that whole system of social relationships on which the development of our personalities depends. Therefore man is saved by being incorporated into the family of God, the fellowship of faith, the body of Christ, and the communion of saints. As this corporate redeemed humanity grows, in extent, unity, and holiness, so is the rest of humanity prepared for incorporation: for humanity is potentially the body of Christ. But as this reintegration of humanity is progressing, so it brings into light a further revelation and presses it upon individual souls, who in turn are brought to a position of greater responsibility, which, if they accept, again helps to influence all humanity; a reciprocating influence of greater power and richer content thus being automatically set up.

(*b*) There is no escaping this developing responsibility. As humanity as a whole depends for its freedom on those who give themselves to fight the battles of liberty, so redeemed humanity depends for its sanctification upon those who consecrate themselves for others' sakes. Thus we are not only dowered with the power of choosing our own salvation, we are dowered with the responsibility of influencing other people's destiny too. Our influence upon others does not go so far as to make the issue whether other souls are saved or lost depend upon us; that responsibility no one can assume for others or escape for himself; but we may hasten or retard the time at which souls may decide upon God's purpose for them; we can prepare souls to receive the fuller light; we can help in the sanctification of humanity. The nature of our choice and the fullness of our acceptance carry with them therefore the earthly happiness of countless souls, and will influence all the future of history.

(*c*) History will be allowed to go on until the highest possibility of corporate redemption is reached.

This is generally spoken of as the making up of God's elect; this means that a certain sufficient number of souls, known only to God, must be united and sanctified that they may be worthy to constitute the body of Christ, each so reflecting the glory of God that the body as a whole may receive enough of the joy and blessedness of God to fulfil His purpose, justify existence, and make reparation for sin and all its consequences. Individual souls will reach different heights of personal sanctity; and from them, those who are beneath them will perceive more of God than they themselves could directly behold. When the general sanctification shall have reached something commensurate to the stature of Christ, then human history will have fulfilled its purpose, no more souls will be created, time will come to an end, and God will be all in all.

3. A critical issue therefore faces the individual soul.

(*a*) Everything must depend upon your decision.

In addition to the fact that God is, and all that He has revealed in the Incarnation and wrought by the Crucifixion; despite the witness of the Church and the work of grace, there must still be your decision. There is no grace that will carry you into the kingdom of heaven without your assent. It may need only a very simple and feeble assent to begin your co-operation, but on that there wait the eternal purpose of God, all the forces of history, and all the grace of Christ. To shirk this decision would mean that you are unwilling to accept the purpose of God, which is that your salvation shall be your own decision; and at every stage of its perfection that decision must be repeated. No doubt there is some critical point at which each soul passes in either direction, never to turn back; where that critical point is no one knows, for some decisions may be reversed. But it is here in this life that the final decision is made; though only beyond this life will it be revealed what that decision has been. For although souls may never have known the Gospel at all, or never have had Christ presented to them in any clear or critical way, there are decisions being made every day that are implicitly decisions of faith or unbelief: decisions that must affect our eternal destiny; and there must come a time when these accumulate, so that direction in one way or the other is finally determined. But as long as one is able to hear the Gospel and understand what it means, the possibility of deciding to accept God's purpose is still open.

(*b*) No one can force the critical hour upon anyone else.

If the preacher of the Gospel could do this, it would

make preaching quite intolerable. The preacher can only say what he knows to be true. He can only discharge his commission, declare the counsel of God, and leave the secrets of all decisions to the soul and its Creator. But it is, of course, possible that, as a result of any clear proclamation of the Gospel, great decisions will be made that will be determinative one way or the other. You may at this very moment decide that you will try to be better, or that you will confess Jesus Christ, or that you will join the Church, or that you will say your prayers more carefully, or that you will use the sacraments; but it is quite possible that the great hour for you has arrived; behind this passing moment there lie the whole of creation's power, the force of evolution, the influences of history, the witness of religion, the testimony of the Church, the prayers of the saints, and beyond it all the Eternal Purpose and the Everlasting Love. At some time or other all these things will bring you to the point where you must make the decision whether or not the purpose of God shall be your purpose too.

(*c*) It is obvious that such a decision must be eternal.

Whenever the whole purpose of God is made known to you in such wise that your mind recognises that it is true, then your heart must decide whether it loves that purpose, and the will whether it will accept it; and the moment this is clearly seen and freely accepted, or freely rejected, the decision must be final, because there is nothing else to be said, there is no other motive to appeal to. And yet we can seek to make known the whole counsel of God to every man, in every possible manner, without fear, knowing that the clearer it is made the more likely it will be that the purpose of God will be chosen.

And so I now declare unto you that all things that have ever been exist for your sake, and that existence was granted you in order that you might embrace the eternal purpose of God, which is that you should know, serve, love, and enjoy Him for ever. The acceptance of this will make your life here, despite sin and sorrow, hardship and hindrance, full of joy and power, and, if maintained, will bring you to everlasting bliss in union with God. That will infinitely justify creation; it is the only explanation of existence, the only worthy end of life; it will alone bring satisfaction to your soul; it is the consummation for which humanity was made.

THE "YEA" OF GOD

THE REV. JOHN SCOTT LIDGETT, M.A., D.D.

Warden of the Bermondsey Settlement since 1891. *Dr. Scott Lidgett was educated at Blackheath Proprietary School, afterwards at University College, London. He entered the Wesleyan ministry in* 1876, *and was stationed successively at Tunstall, Southport, Cardiff, Wolverhampton, and Cambridge. He founded, in connection with the late Dr. Moulton, the Bermondsey Settlement in* 1891. *He became President of the National Council of the Evangelical Free Churches of England and Wales in* 1906, *and Hon. Joint Secretary in* 1914; *President of the Wesleyan Methodist Conference,* 1908; *President of the Free Church Commission,* 1912–15; *Member of the Royal Commission on Venereal Diseases,* 1913–15; *Leader of the Progressive Party on the L.C.C. since* 1918. *Amongst his publications are: "The Spiritual Principle of the Atonement," "The Fatherhood of God in Christian Truth and Life," "The Christian Religion: its Meaning and Proof," "Apostolic Ministry," "God in Christ Jesus: a Study of St. Paul's Epistle to the Ephesians," "Sonship and Salvation, A Study of the Epistle to the Hebrews," "God, Christ, and the Church."*

THE "YEA" OF GOD

BY THE REV. J. SCOTT LIDGETT, D.D.

"*For how many soever be the promises of God, in Him is the yea; wherefore also through Him is the Amen, unto the glory of God through us.*"—2 Cor. i. 20.

ST. PAUL is a difficult writer. Many of the forms of thought and reasoning by which he satisfied his own difficulties and sought to meet those of his contemporaries create, rather than solve, difficulties for us. Yet whenever he reaches the highest realities of the Faith and expresses the inmost experiences of the spirit, he strikes a universal note, which is as modern as it is ancient. So it is with the declaration of our text.

In order to understand this great saying, we must start by putting ourselves at the Apostle's point of view. It is fully explained to us at the outset of this Epistle. Although St. Paul's spiritual experience was profoundly and intensely personal, he had been completely set free from all the limitations of self-interested individualism. He had just passed through almost overwhelming sufferings, both physical and mental. These sufferings had been made more poignant by the acute and delicate sensibility which, as in the case of Jeremiah, was inextricably bound up with his adamantine strength. He had "despaired even of life." Yet God, by His abundant comfort, had delivered him "out of so great a death." His courage and confidence, his hope and expectation, had thereby been fully restored. He was himself again, and more than himself since his weakness had been reinforced by the life-giving succour and empowerment of God. For what purpose was this humiliation and exaltation? Not for his own sake merely. It was in order that he might "be able to comfort them that are in any affliction, through the comfort wherewith we are comforted by God." Thus his sufferings had been an overflow of the sufferings of Christ, in order that both they and the comfort which had restored him might be taken up into the redemptive ministry of Christ to the Church. This particular experience of the Apostle sprang out of that complete union of his inmost personality with Christ which enabled him to say, "To me to live is Christ." Hence this complete and mystic union constrained him so to base all his life on Christ that Divine reality and loftiest truth not only inspired his motives and shaped his purposes, but even dictated all the details of his conduct throughout his ministry to the Church.

Here was a case in point. His incapacitating affliction had delayed his promised visit to Corinth. He had also been held back by his anxiety to receive reassuring tidings about the condition of the Church, so that his visit might be one of encouraging fellowship, and not of fault-finding and correction. This delay had either been taken advantage of by his enemies, or had aroused his apprehension that it would be so taken advantage of. He would be accounted a Yea-and-Nay man, whose character was fickle, whose purposes were unstable, and whose promises were untrustworthy. Such changeableness was impossible and even unthinkable. His character and conduct must needs be an expression of the positiveness and steadfastness of his Lord. The trustworthiness of Christ had been, and must be, made manifest in the trustworthiness of His Apostle. The Son of God, as preached by him and his companions, had not been " Yea and Nay," but a consistent and all-embracing " Yea." " For how many soever be the promises of God, in Him is the yea." The certitude and positiveness of Christ impose certitude and positiveness upon His servant, whose life must needs be, both in word and deed, a revelation of his Lord. And more. The certitude and positiveness of Christ, the Son of God, are the final and convincing guarantee of the trustworthiness of God. The fulfilment of His promises, in all their infinite variety and amplitude, is assured by the fact and presence of Christ, His Son.

Thus, as it seems to me, a wonderful vision arises before the mind of the Apostle. Mankind, represented by the Church, is gathered together in the presence of the Unseen. The countless promises of God are called to mind and recited. The assembly awaits in tensest expectation the assurance that they hold good and will be fulfilled. Suddenly before their awestruck gaze appears the Son of God. In Him—His Personality and His Presence—is emblazoned the satisfying " Yea " of God. And immediately there bursts from the waiting congregation the " Amen " of confident faith and hope, of joyful and devout acceptance, not only of the assurance, but of the actual gift and bestowal of God in Christ. He brings to men the Revelation and Redemption of God in such wise as to give such assurance of the order and destiny of the world as satisfies the needs and hopes of men.

I. It was inevitable that St. Paul should think in

terms of Divine promises and their fulfilment, for expectancy was of the very essence of Old Testament religion. Yet in this respect, as in others, Old Testament Revelation and Jewish religion give precise point and expression to what is universal in the method of God and in the corresponding temper of mankind.

Man, as well as Revelation, comes into being by means of and under the influence of promises. The doctrine of evolution is not an *explanation* of the universe, but it is the best description, at present available, of the method by which it has come and is still coming into being. The unfolding of the Divine purpose is contained in the slow and costly upbuilding of the world. Gradualness is inevitable in respect both of nature and of man. And this involves not merely the Divine creation, but the creaturely self-building of the world. Above all is this co-operation of the Creator and the creature to be found throughout the realm of consciousness—the spiritual world. The future is forecast and brought about by means of human ideals, which are given to men as their starting-point, carrying such a measure of assurance with them as arouses confident hope and inspires sustained effort. Such ideals and their attendant hopes are instinctively treated as revealing something of the nature and meaning of the universe, of the mind and will of God.

Hence man comes into being, not merely with a sense of dependence, but as an actively responsible and expectant being. He seeks not only being, but better-being; demands not merely security of existence, but the satisfaction that makes continued existence worth while. "We are saved by hope," says St. Paul elsewhere. The place and worth of any civilisation is measured by the elevation and extent of its hopes, and by its assurance—even if it be only instinctive—that the order of things, that God, is pledged to such fulfilment of them as will justify it to Reason, with its spiritual aspirations and moral demands. The sign of healthy manhood everywhere is that Faith and Hope, as the expression of Love, cast out fear, that expectancy overcomes and expels apprehension.

It is essential that this fact should be borne in mind at a time when the Great War with its consequences overshadows the mind and oppresses the heart of man. The mystery of suffering weighs heavily upon us, so much so that an eminent Christian thinker has recently declared that "Pain is the fundamental fact in life." [1] Yet whatever may be said of life, it is certainly not true that pain is the fundamental fact of *consciousness*, whether animal or human. And it is consciousness that counts. The attraction of hope is more universal and more effective than the pressure of pain, though the spur of pain is a useful but subordinate ally of the incitement of hope. This consideration is of the utmost importance when we are told that "Darwin's triumph has destroyed the whole theological scheme," and that man, so far from having fallen "from an ideal state of perfect innocence," is "an animal slowly gaining spiritual understanding" and with the gain "rising far above his distant ancestors." [2] The divergence between the new and the old is not so serious if it be borne in mind that the consciousness of resistance to the authority

[1] Canon Streeter, in his book entitled *Reality*, p. 57.

[2] By the Bishop of Birmingham in Westminster Abbey, September 25, 1927.

of the higher carries with it the sense of a Fall, although the very capacity of experiencing this consciousness implies a rise in the scale of being—the attainment of responsible manhood. Hence there is a spring of possibilities and hope within the Fall. "The seed of woman shall bruise the serpent's head" was the promise that, according to the narrative of Genesis, succeeded the transgression and its condemnation. Redemption, therefore, must be seen as consisting not so much in reparation of the past as in fulfilment of the future. Fulfilment is the way of reparation, the fulfilment of "the promises of God" which have from the beginning prevented the failures and the Fall of man from being complete and irretrievable. Redemption comes through the gift and influence of the "promises."

II. Men have been, and are still being, led forward by the appeal of a vast range of promises that rest upon faith and awaken hope. They embrace and appeal to every human interest and concern, from those of mere animal life onward to the highest aims of civilisation. They give some degree of elevation even to the pursuit of the material. Yet there have come to men throughout their history intuitions and yearnings, hopes and demands, which have suggested with irresistible influence and have partially revealed the existence and presence of a higher order, eternal and divine, by which the present order of things, with all its lower values, must be estimated and judged. Visions of Truth, Beauty, and Goodness have been vouchsafed, which have called forth the awe-stricken sense of the Holy, the conviction, to use the words of Martineau, that "when the secret of the universe is disclosed, it will not be found to be profane." Such visions have come, first of all, to the prophets and the poets, the seers and mystics of mankind, and through them have become the spiritual heritage of ordinary men. These intimations make their authority and influence felt, not amid the rush of life, but in its still hours and its solemnising experiences. The mark of "given-ness" attends such visions and intimations. They come from above, and not from beneath or around. They claim authority, create higher and holier standards, awaken expectancy. They become the satisfying ends by which the meaning and worth of the universe and of human life are henceforth judged. They are "the pearl of great price" for the sake of which the merchantman "seeking goodly pearls" will part with all that he has. They are "promises of God," and in their presence all other promises of life, however innocent or even essential they may be, sink to secularity. Upon the trustworthiness of these intimations and upon their fulfilment the salvation and satisfaction of mankind depend. Failing such fulfilment, the nature and government of the universe are a baffling enigma, for if they should prove illusory the universe has been the birthplace and spring of spiritual ideals and aspirations to which it is indifferent, although they are so essential to the making of man that only the influence of the highest can safeguard and foster the lowliest. Their fulfilment is as necessary to the collective well-being of the race as to the goodness of individual men.

These "promises of God" and their fulfilment had been the special concern of the Hebrew prophets. Their messages of hope and expectancy were chiefly—though in view of the breadth of his insight and sympathies not exclusively—in the Apostle's mind.

The distinctiveness of "the promises of God" as announced by the Hebrew prophets is fourfold.

In the first place they carry an authoritative assurance of their fulfilment. "These things shall be."

In the next place, while profoundly spiritual, they embrace the universe within their scope, and witness to its wholeness. They announce a "far-off Divine event, to which the whole creation moves." They conceive this event as a *setting right* of all things. Above all, they ground the certainty and amplitude of this fulfilment not upon the needs and desires of men, but on the character of God. They proclaim "the righteousness of God" as the guarantee of the spiritual hopes of man. What God is contains the explanation of what He is doing, the promise of what He will do.

The "promises of God" are many and manifold. In presence of them the Apostle abandons his love of precise definition. "*However many soever* be the promises of God," he says, just as elsewhere he speaks of the "trackless" riches of Christ. "The kingdom of God" is not the assertion of His supreme and all-commanding will, but the outcome of His self-imparting grace. The manifestation of God will achieve and confer the blessedness of man, the complete satisfaction of spiritual demands, which God has Himself inbreathed as the earnest of their final satisfaction.

The Fatherhood of God implies that He is "the God of hope" in order that He may be "the God of peace." Upon the making good of His promises it depends whether man shall become more than an animal, though a rational animal, and shall come into the fullness of his manhood by living "not by bread alone," assisted by all the complicated machinery that security and sufficiency of bread involve, "but by every word that proceedeth out of the mouth of God."

III. Where, then, is the assurance of this fulfilment to be found? "In Him"—that is in Christ, the Son of God—"is the yea." The fact of Christ is the only, it is also the convincing and satisfying, guarantee of the faithfulness, the trustworthiness of God. Accept the reality and the significance of Christ, and all is assured. Deny Him, or disparage Him, and all is lost. "He that followeth Me," He says, "shall not walk in darkness, but shall have the light of life."

The secret of Christ was, above all, that He Himself completely enjoyed this "light of life," that He lived in the unbroken and immediate consciousness of the reality, the presence, the fellowship of God as His Father. This consciousness gave to Him alike His dauntless serenity and command of circumstances, the boundless energy of His beneficence, the fullness of His beatitude. Through it He transformed suffering into sacrifice, defeat into triumph, death into resurrection. For Him enjoyment transcended expectancy. The love of God became the wellspring of His incomparable human life.

Fulfilment is the essential quality of Christ—of His personality, His work, and His influence. He confirms the promises of God to mankind by fulfilling in Himself the ideal of manhood in its relations with God. The highest principle of life, according to John Stuart Mill, is "so to act that Jesus Christ would approve of your life." Even His Cross was not a defeat, nor merely an expiation. It was the fulfilment and therefore the restoration, through sacrificial obedience, of the ideal of which sin is either the defiant or the careless contradiction.

And what He Himself enjoyed, that He also conveyed to His followers, giving to them a new knowledge of God and a new power over the world. He bore away their sin, transformed their impotence, bequeathed to them His Spirit. He brought them into the main-stream of the redemptive and renewing energies of the Divine life and love. And all this is the earnest of what He has been and will be to all those who surrender themselves to Him and accept His "Yea" to all the promises of God. The "Yea" of God is for ever spoken in the historic fact of Christ, the Son of God, the Saviour of men. His historicity is vital, for while the "promises of God" may be ideal, the "Yea" that confirms them must be actual. Take Christ and all that He stands for, inspires, and satisfies, out of the world, and with His withdrawal the entire fabric of ideal truth, beauty, and goodness is shaken to its base.

IV. What, then, should be the response? Surely, "the Amen" of worshipful acceptance, of confident and joyful trust, in which the faith of individual believers swells and is sustained by the chorus of the Church. Such faith is a venture of hope, inspired by love. Yet this venture is as completely justified in the spiritual world as is a response to the light, and to the world that is illuminated by it, in the natural world. For the reality and promise of the spiritual world is bound up with the reality and gift of Christ.

Never has there been an age when "the promises of God" made such a many-sided appeal to the hopes of men. The ideals of international peace, of social righteousness, of personal well-being, demand their fulfilment, not merely for the satisfaction, but even for the survival of mankind. Yet the ancient cry is repeated, "The children are come to the birth, and there is not strength to bring forth." Man's spiritual inadequacy has compelled a Bishop[1] to ask Science to stay its hand until man is good enough to be trusted with the powers it confers, and a historian to conclude his narrative by the gloomy observation that "In the earlier scene, man's impotence to contend with nature made his life brutish and brief. To-day his very command over nature, so admirably and marvellously won, has become his greatest peril."[2]

Yet, if men will but say "Amen" to the "Yea" of Christ, the danger will be surmounted and the promised good will be well within man's reach. The salvation of mankind, personal and collective, in every realm of human concern, depends upon the vision and acceptance of "Jesus only."

[1] The Bishop of Ripon in a sermon before the British Association, 1927.
[2] G. M. Trevelyan in his *History of England*, p. 703.

KING FOR EVER

THE BISHOP OF LONDON

The Right Hon. and Right Rev. Arthur Foley Winnington Ingram, K.C.V.O. (*cr.* 1915), *D.D., LL.D.; Dean of the Chapels Royal since* 1901; *Prelate of the Order of the British Empire*, 1918; *b. Worcestershire, January* 26, 1858; *fourth son of the Rev. E. Winnington Ingram, Stamford Rectory and Ribbesford House, and Louisa, d. of Right Rev. Bishop Pepys, Worcester; unmarried. Educ. Marlborough College and Keble College, Oxford. First class Mods., second class Greats, Oxford. Private tutor*, 1881–4; *Curate at St. Mary's, Shrewsbury*, 1884–5; *Private Chaplain to Bishop of Lichfield*, 1885–9; *Head of Oxford House, Bethnal Green, Chaplain to Archbishop of York and to Bishop of St. Albans*, 1889; *Rector of Bethnal Green*, 1895; *Rural Dean of Spitalfields*, 1896; *Canon of St. Paul's Cathedral*, 1897–1901; *Bishop of Stepney (Suffragan to Bishop of London)*, 1897–1901; *Chaplain London Rifle Brigade since* 1901; *Chaplain N.A.V.R.; Grand Cross of the Royal Order of the Redeemer*, 1919; *St. Sava*, 1*st Class*, 1919. *Publications:* "*Work in Great Cities*"; "*Old Testament Difficulties*"; "*New Testament Difficulties*"; "*Church Difficulties*"; "*Messengers, Watchmen, Stewards*"; "*The Men who Crucify Christ*," 1896; "*Christ and His Friends*," 1897; "*Banners of the Christian Faith*," 1899; "*The Church in Time of War*," 1915; "*The Potter and the Clay*," 1917; "*Rays of Dawn*," 1918; "*Victory and After*," 1919; "*The Spirit of Peace*," 1921.

KING FOR EVER

BY THE BISHOP OF LONDON

"*The Lord sitteth above the water-flood: the Lord remaineth the King for ever.*"—Ps. xxix. 9–10.

IF I only had one sermon to preach I think I should concentrate the mind of my congregation upon the touching picture of our Lord standing above the hungry multitude; everybody is making to Him suggestions, some of them very foolish ones, but He is quite calm Himself, because "He Himself knows what He will do."

Now, the reason why I think this is such a striking picture is because we believe that the same Person who stood above the multitude in those far-off days stands above the multitude to-day. With all our difficulties in London with regard to housing the poor, feeding the great population, and above all spiritually feeding them, it is our great comfort to think that our Lord is as near to us to-day as He was to those people years ago, that He takes as deep an interest in them, and that though we are much perplexed as to what to do, He Himself "knows what He will do," and therefore I should take for the text of my one and only sermon the last two verses of the 29th Psalm, verses 9 and 10: "The Lord sitteth above the water-flood, the Lord remaineth a King for ever."

Now let us see what this means in detail. Notice the whole point is that it is not some vague God who is above everything, but the actual Person whom we read about in the New Testament and whom we seem to know so well. It is said of Jesus Christ that all authority has been given unto him in Heaven and in earth, and therefore it is Jesus Christ Himself who sits above the water-flood and remains a King for ever. Now, first of all, what does this not mean and what does it mean ?

I. What does it not mean ?

(1) It does not mean that we are not to use our *brains*. It is a common delusion that if we are Christians we are to think as little as possible, that if we think too much we shall lose our faith. Whereas what we want people to do is to think and read a great deal more than they do. As Bacon says, " A little knowledge inclineth man's mind to atheism, but much knowledge brings his mind back to religion." He cannot therefore read or think too much about religion. We must investigate all the reasons why we should believe, face all new discoveries, in science, history, or higher criticism, believing that " we can do nothing against the truth but for the truth."

(2) We have to use our *hearts*. It is said that St. John when he was a very old man used to be carried into church, and that all he was able to say was, " Little children, love one another." He could not have said anything more to the point, for all our difficulties in life to-day spring from want of Christian love. It is want of confidence in one another among the nations which hold matters up at Geneva ; it is want of confidence between employer and employee which produces most of our industrial troubles ; in parishes it is jealousy between workers which upsets many a parish ; and how many homes, which would otherwise be happy,

are made miserable by the want of true love! And therefore we have to use our hearts.

(3) We have to use our *hands.* It is not always realised that, as Mr. Holland so forcibly said to us at the Guildhall at a great missionary meeting, we are the *only* Body Christ has on earth. We are actually His hands and feet, and if we don't stretch out our hands, according to His plan, He can't stretch out His hand. If our foot doesn't move, He cannot go. If our lips do not open, He cannot speak; and therefore hands and feet and lips must be freely used.

(4) We have to use our *wills.* It is almost amusing, if it were not sad, to hear those who disown religion pose as the only people who use their wills: "I will be master of my fate, I will be captain of my soul," as Henley says. But as a matter of fact every Christian has to use his will to the uttermost. The boy who stands up at his Confirmation and says "I do" has got to put all his determination into keeping his promise. None of us will ever conquer our besetting sin without exercising the power of our wills. The sad reason why we are not better is because we do not really *will* to be, and therefore brain, heart, hands, and will have to be used just as if there were no Lord sitting above the water-flood.

II. But now comes the second question: Where does religion come in? What does this picture of our Lord standing above the multitude really mean to us? Let us take each one of those four points one by one.

(1) Take our *brains.* It means that when we have thought and read and reasoned and asked the advice

of our friends, we have one more glorious privilege, we can kneel down, and look up and say :

> Come, Holy Ghost, our souls inspire,
> And lighten with celestial fire ;
> Thou the anointing Spirit art,
> Who dost thy sevenfold gifts impart.

In other words, we can have what the Prayer Book calls "the heavenly assistance of the Holy Ghost." It is the task of the Holy Spirit to take of Christ and show Him to us, and thus we have conveyed to our minds the advice of Him who knows what He would do. This is such a priceless privilege that it is perfectly astonishing that so many do not avail themselves of it. It seems almost mad to start a day on which we have so many decisions to make without asking for the guidance of this Divine Guide.

(2) Then take our *hearts*. Mere good-nature soon comes to an end. Our limited supply of human love is nothing like enough to solve the problems of the world. I met in Japan a lady who has worked for thirty years among the lepers. Do you suppose that it was merely human love which has carried her on for so long ? Where religion comes in, is that it enables us to place our poor hearts alongside of the heart of the Good Shepherd, who is still the Good Shepherd, although he is King. Our hearts therefore can beat with the throb of His heart, and we can love with His love. "I can't love those people naturally," said a priest to me once ; "Then you must love them supernaturally," I said in reply. Nothing is more striking than the way in which a man or woman's capacity for loving increases as time goes on.

(3) Then we turn to where religion comes in as we work with *our hands and feet and lips.* The promise is given that we shall not work alone; the Lord, we are told, was working with those first disciples, and was "confirming the Word with signs following." When I was alone for nine years working in East London and finding comparatively few respond at first to my efforts, that was my great comfort. Christ asks my work, but not my success. I have to do my best, but He takes the responsibility Himself. This is the comfort of every lonely worker throughout the world.

(4) Then when we come to our *wills*, religion comes in in this way. When the young boy or weak girl make their promise and then asked for help to keep it, there comes down upon their wills a *great strong Hand* which closes round their wills like a bar of steel, and in that new power they can do what they could not possibly do by themselves. This is why we see young boys and girls standing firm under difficulties which seem, humanly speaking, bound to overwhelm them.

III. Let us see in conclusion how this affects various parts of our lives.

(1) It affects our *prayer life.* If the very Person who said, "Ask, and ye shall have; seek, and ye shall find," is at the centre of all things, then it becomes absolutely certain that prayer will be answered, because the very Person who tells us to pray will give the answer to that prayer.

(2) So, again, notice the encouragement it gives to *intercession.* We are told that our Lord ever liveth to make intercession for us, and therefore our weak

intercessions get swept into His all-prevailing intercession. As the hymn says:

> What, fallen again? yet cheerful rise,
> Thy Intercessor never dies.

(3) See what an inspiration it is to a *life of service*. If Christ, according to His plan, cannot do without us, then we must be up and doing. It is only a glorious privilege to offer our hands and feet and lips for His service.

(4) And lastly, it ought to take away from us all fear of *death*. Death to us, as it was to St. Paul, ought only to be "to depart and be with Christ, which is far better." And therefore you see my one sermon would promise to me, and also, I hope, to others, strength and hope and grace in this life, and in the world to come life everlasting.

FINALITY IN OUR DEALINGS WITH GOD

THE REV. FREDERICK BROTHERTON MEYER, B.A., D.D.

Dr. Meyer was educated at Brighton College and Regent's Park Baptist College. He became Assistant Minister to the Rev. C. M. Birrell, at Liverpool, in 1870. *Two years later he was called to the Baptist Chapel, York, and still later to Leicester, where the Melbourne Hall was built for his ministry. He has been pastor to the Regent's Park Chapel, London, and also Christ Church, Westminster Bridge Road, of which he has been Minister Emeritus since* 1921. *In* 1904 *and* 1920 *he was President of the National Federation of Free Churches, and also of the Baptist Union in* 1906. *He is the author of the following: "Israel: a Prince with God," "Elijah," "Tried by Fire," "The Bells of Is," "Reveries and Realities," "Workaday Sermons," "Blessed are Ye."*

FINALITY IN OUR DEALINGS WITH GOD

BY THE REV. F. B. MEYER, D.D.

"*Not as though I had already attained, either were already perfect.*"—Phil. iii. 12.

GOD is Love! But love demands love! It is a necessary condition of love that there should be reciprocity. Probably, therefore, the human race was created in the image of God that there might be an adequate response to the Heart of the Eternal —not yet, except in a few instances, but finally, when our eternal experiences have matured our characters. "*Now* are we the sons of God, and it doth not yet appear what we shall be."

The suggestion has been hazarded that God's choice of our young race may have led to the jealous hatred of angels who were passed over. For verily, not of angels did He take hold. Out of this arose the great revolt of which the Earth has been, and is, the scene —the scene of the worst, but destined to be the cradle of the best.

It was the opinion of the late Dr. Wallace that this tiny planet is the only inhabited bit of star-dust amid the myriads of the midnight sky; and it may be that this is the chosen nursery for the testing and education of those who shall become the sons and daughters of the Almighty. Certainly the events which have taken place here—the Incarnation, Death, Resurrection, and Ascension of Jesus Christ—have for ever signalised our earth amid all other worlds, and it is not incredible that it is serving as the testing-place and the school of those who shall compose the Church or Group of the First-Born.

I. The Divine Ideals which Appeal for our Attainment

Each one of us is created within reach of a glorious destiny. We may be the sons and daughters of the Almighty in no fictitious sense! Heirs of God and joint heirs with His Son! Is it wonderful, therefore, that we should receive, from the shifting events of time and sense, the special training needed for the future which awaits us? In the children of a large family there is a vast diversity of character, and happy are those parents who can afford to give each child that education which is most suited to develop its idiosyncrasy. So each unit of humanity is a distinct creation. Each incarnates some distinct thought of the Creator, and the life-career of each is specially arranged and determined to develop the special characteristics of each. God never repeats Himself. Each soul in Eph. ii. 10 is compared to a poem. No poet repeats himself. Each production bears trace of some new aspect of consummate art. There may be similarity, but there can be no identity. Each of us, therefore, enshrines a distinct ideal of God's mind, but we have to *work out* our own salvation with fear and trembling. We have to apprehend that for which we were apprehended by Christ Jesus. And we are placed in this world for a brief space that we may work out what God is working in, and approximate so far as possible to the Divine ideal. Perhaps each one of us, before birth, stands before the Creator and Father, to see the ideal of what we may become. This is the haunting thought which we know as conscience; and which reproaches us each time when we fall short. It is also the inspiration of a nobler career. As Moses, on the summit of Sinai, beheld in the vision the pattern of the Tabernacle which he was to construct, and it stood there in radiant beauty, every knot and tassel, every curtain and fringe, every pillar and hook, perfectly reflected as from the Divine thought, so it may be that each of us at that sublime moment beheld at a glance the vision of what God had apprehended us to become.

In some cases the pattern is only revealed step by step and day by day. Each morning the Spirit of God presents to us some new item in the Divine conception, and summons us to realise it. Thus the Temple groweth into a dwelling-place for the Eternal, or a chosen servant as Moses became. The one particular which we are stressing now is that our lives have been forecasted. There was a reason for our creation. God thought a distinct thought into our souls, as they issued from the womb of creation. Perhaps a record has been kept in the archives of eternity, with which we shall compare what life has actually been! Is not this an incentive that we should follow on to apprehend that for which we were apprehended? Let us follow on!

II. The Divine Ideal or Purpose can only be Realised in Stages

"Not that I have already attained, or am already made perfect; but I press on." It is, as Paul says, "a high calling." It is also described as "a holy calling," "a heavenly calling," and "a hope-inspiring calling." The wireless telegraphy of God's Spirit is ever bringing that call to mind, unless the obstinacy of man's refusal deadens the voice to a far-off whisper that presently ceases. If only our ears were attent, we should detect the low, sweet voice of God, nearer, clearer, stronger, intenser, more thrilling, more eager. But it calls for each single step or act in our response to be taken separately and deliberately. We go from strength to strength. We leave the things that are behind, and reach out towards those before. As there are rings in the centre of a tree, so that the woodsman can decipher the years of growth, so there are distinct stages in our progress towards the Divine ideal. It is probable that each faithful soul is standing before the ascent of the Eternal.

A friend discovered Thorwaldsen in tears, and on asking the reason the illustrious sculptor replied: "Look at that statue. I have reached my ideal, and fear that I have reached the high-water mark of my profession. When a man is satisfied, he ceases to grow." How different this is to the cry of the Apostle. Not only did he press on through obloquy and reproach, through imprisonment and stripes, through the persecution of the Jews and the martyrdom under Nero, but from the excellent glory into which he has passed we seem to hear those same triumphant notes: "I am pressing on." From the distant height Longfellow's mountain-climber's voice was still heard crying "Excelsior!" So must it be with us, and our behaviour in every fresh incident of life shall conduce to the achievement of our life-purpose. Never counting ourselves to have attained or to be already perfect. Never deterred by the amazing difficulties through which, and notwithstanding which, we pursue our way. Never weary in submitting to those inward strivings of the Spirit, those birth-pangs of new and holier attainments, to which the saints of God are exposed. "Groanings that cannot be uttered."

We must learn to forget! We are all tempted to live in the past, to look up at the fading laurels we have won, as though they could not be equalled or surpassed, to confess that we shall never do anything so good as that, never reach so high, never paint so fair a picture, preach so good a sermon, have such a vision of God! That is fatal. Forget! Forget the rapture of your first Communion, the earliest efforts of your soul, the trophies you won, the visions of truth, the mountain-top experience, and press onward, upward, with the eagle's flight to the sun!

III. The Realisation of the Soul's Ideals is only Possible when there is Finality in our Dealings with God

The failure, in a vast number of lives, arises from our lack of understanding of the prime law of growth, truly envisaged by the Apostle when he speaks of "leaving those things which are behind." There are stages in the Christian's growth; rings, as we have said, in the tree; crease-marks on the grass; cairns left behind in the march. There must, in fact, be definite and final dealings with the past, with conscience, and with God.

In the mystic ladder, trodden by holy souls in all ages, there are these successive stages, each of which must be definitely approached, appropriated, and passed. There must be a definite crossing of the Equator, not once in a lifetime, but in many succeeding experiences. When once the step is taken, and the contract made between the soul and God, there should be a sense of Finality. The first step has been taken, and need not be retaken. That apartment in the house is furnished, and need not take attention from the rest. That lesson has been definitely learned and passed. That goal has been attained; there is no need even to dwell on it, otherwise than as a settled matter between God and the soul. *This only must be borne in mind, that such definite steps must be ratified and settled with the Divine endorsement. The final act is one of faith that God has definitely accepted and ratified the act, and has set His seal of affirmation upon it.* The step is taken in faith! Then the Divine Spirit enables us to reckon that He has accepted and endorsed it. From that time onward the soul advances with unwavering faith. That purpose is achieved once and for ever. That stage at least has been gained, and needs never to be reconsidered.

Let us now take three illustrations of finality in the soul's progress. *First: the consciousness that, on our confession, sin is absolutely forgiven and put away.* I remember an interview with an elderly man in which he told me that every night before he slept he confessed all the sins of the past that he could recall, and sought forgiveness. Obviously such an ordeal was arduous, costly of sleep and rest, and altogether unnecessary, in face of the continual affirmations of Scripture. The statements on page after page are clear as crystal. "*As far as the east is from the west, so far hath He removed our transgression.*" "*I, even I, am He that blotteth out thy transgressions, and will no more remember thy sins.*" "*Thou wilt cast all their sins into the depth of the seas.*" "*If we confess our sins, He is faithful and just to forgive us our sins, and to cleanse us.*" Nothing could be more explicit and definite. When I had quoted these assurances to my companion, I went on to show him the grave injustice he was committing, not only against himself, but against the Eternal Lover. Surely God's repeated assurance is enough, and more than enough!

There may come a definite moment when the soul faces its past, and in true penitence returns, prodigal-like, to the Father, with the frank confession of the past. As soon as the frank and full confession has been made, the whole black record is obliterated. Nothing of the past will ever be mentioned again. It is forgiven and forgotten from that hour; and it must be a grievous hurt to the Divine Spirit to be asked again and again to forgive. What would any of us think if our children, having been forgiven for some breach of righteousness, were to come morning after morning to implore forgiveness? In this grave issue surely God demands, and we should reckon on, finality. Once confessed and forgiven, our sins can no more be recovered than a pebble cast into the depths of the Atlantic. That matter being settled once and for ever, it can be left behind for ever, and the same finality must be claimed as we may be overcome in secret or overt sin.

The same attitude should be adopted in regard to Divine guidance. There are three steps whch enable us to come to a definite conclusion as to our life-course, and the demands for decision and choice of route, which arise from time to time. As a general rule, there are three steps. In the first place, a resolve or sense of duty begins to form in the secret depths of the soul. It is a still small voice, speaking in the Horeb of the heart. A whisper! A suggestion! A question! At this stage we are wise not to mention it to the dearest, closest friend! Ask that, if it be not of God, it may die away! But if it grows, nurture it, expose it to the scrutiny of the Divine Spirit, and watch for the corroboration of outward circumstances. The inward and outward will correspond as did the incidents on that memorable day in Saul's life, which corroborated Samuel's secret anointing; and as the shut doors along the coast of Asia Minor compelled Paul to take the ship to Europe. Finally, there will be corroboration on the part of those whom at this stage we consult. When these three signs agree, we must dare to roll the entire responsibility on God's Providence, as Abraham did, when he left Haran and flung himself into the desert which intervened between the Euphrates and Damascus. "He went out, not knowing whither he went." But he never returned, and God vindicated him. Similarly men, as individuals or in groups, have stepped forth on unknown paths; but when faith takes a step of that nature, whatever be the difficulties and perils, there must be no looking back. The responsibility for all the future must be cast on God. He must and will provide. The crooked shall be made straight, and the rough places smooth. Manna shall distil on the desert floor, and rocks shall break into fountains, because God also respects the finality which characterises the pilgrim soul, that makes the humble compact, and steps forth in faith.

The same attitude should be adopted in the presence of a heavy sorrow, which ever lies on the heart and extorts sighs and tears. It is natural to entreat that the cup should be taken away, and that the long discipline should cease. It is natural to return day after day and night after night to that same spot in our Gethsemane, to bedew the same sward with sweat of blood, and lament on the air the same petitions. But there must come an end to this, if we would follow in the footsteps of our Lord. We must accept the discipline as the Divine will, whether it be imposed or permitted. We must believe that God has a definite purpose and reason in regard to it. We must come to the point of definitely accepting it as the Father's choice for us. We must tell Him of our willingness to suffer so long as He deems it to be necessary. We may ask for an angel to strengthen us, but we must allow our wrists to be bound with thongs. Thus, quietly waiting, the sky will begin to brighten in the east; the lesson will have been learnt; the blessing which could only accrue in this manner will be granted. The definite acceptance of some heavy cross, without murmuring or complaining, but simply trusting, with the upward glance and smile, and with the quiet acquiescence of the soul, is not only the way of peace, but must be more pleasing to God than the querulous complaint and the prolonged entreaty for release. God has no pleasure in our pain. It grieves Him when we are passing through the dark valley. Jesus must have suffered acutely whilst He abode two days in the place where He was till Lazarus died, that in that beloved home He might perform His greatest miracle. Reckon God as your partner in sorrow, and leave to Him the hour and method of your deliverance.

The only experience in our mortal life in which we cannot always claim finality is in our intercession for others. " God forbid," said the patriot-prophet, " that I should sin against the Lord in ceasing to pray for you." But even in this case the soul may become assured that the prayer has been answered, and then the prayer is turned to praise, and the intercessor quietly waits to see the salvation of God. Intercession, like that recorded of our Lord in John xvi, can never cease. " He ever liveth to make intercession."

Scripture abounds with instances of finality in dealing with God. Samuel's mother, having poured out her heart, was no more sad. The nobleman who came to Christ for his child, instead of waiting for further assurance, believed the word that Jesus spake, and went his way! The sailors and crew were so reassured by Paul's prayer and vision that they dared to empty the ship of the cargo of wheat. Why should not we cast our burdens on the Lord, and leave them there, without fear as to the result, when once we have the inner conviction that God has accepted us? Never in this life shall we feel that we have apprehended all for which we have been apprehended. Always will new experiences beckon you, like higher mountain-reaches. Always leave things behind, and press on, and take this for your comfort, that you have been apprehended by God for your quest, and He will not fail you. It is related of the great artist Herkomer that his aged father lived in his home and spent his days in modelling clay. At night he placed the day's work on the shelf with a sigh as he detected the effect of the pilfering years. But when he had retired to the early bed of age, his gifted son entered the workshop, took up one by one the objects over which his father lamented, touched them with inimitable skill, and the old man, as he took them up in the morning, dismissed the regrets of the previous night, and said delightedly, " After all, I can do as well as ever." So at the end of life, and often during life, when we confess that we have not apprehended, we shall discover that Christ's deft touch has perfected our poor handiwork.

THE ETERNAL VALUES

THE VERY REV. WILLIAM RALPH INGE, D.D., C.V.O., F.B.A.

Dean of St. Paul's. Dean Inge is the eldest son of the late Rev. William Inge, D.D., Provost of Worcester College, Oxford, and of Mary, daughter of the Ven. Edward Churton, Archdeacon of Cleveland. Educated at Eton and passing on to King's College, Cambridge, he gained many distinctions, becoming Senior Chancellor's Medallist in 1883 *and Hare Prizeman in* 1885. *He was formerly Assistant Master at Eton; Fellow and Tutor of Hertford College, Oxford; Lady Margaret Professor of Divinity and Hon. Fellow of Jesus College, Cambridge. He has been Select Preacher at both Oxford and Cambridge, and has been successively chosen as Bampton Lecturer; Paddock Lecturer, New York; Gifford Lecturer, St. Andrews; and Romanes and Hibbert Lecturer. Amongst his publications are: "Christian Mysticism," "The Philosophy of Plotinus," "Outspoken Essays," "The Idea of Progress," "The Victorian Age."*

THE ETERNAL VALUES

BY THE VERY REV. W. R. INGE, D.D.

"*When I consider Thy heavens, the work of Thy fingers, the moon and the stars, which Thou hast ordained; what is man, that Thou art mindful of him? and the son of man, that thou visitest him?*"—Ps. viii. 3, 4.

THE contrast between the starry heavens and the puny dwellers on this earth is far more tremendous than the Psalmist knew it to be. His universe was a small one compared with that which we contemplate. And yet the disproportion seemed to him almost crushing. But not quite. For man is, after all, "the roof and crown of things," at least within our knowledge. "Thou hast made him to have dominion over the works of Thine hands; thou hast put all things in subjection under his feet." So the old Hebrew poet, like the philosopher Kant, finds two things in the world worthy of awe and wonder—the heavens above, and the moral nature of man within him.

The tendency to worship the sun, moon, and stars has been widespread, and is easy to understand. Even the later Greek philosophers, after the longest period of unfettered speculation that the human race has ever enjoyed, still thought that the worlds have souls, higher in rank than those of human individuals. The eminent philosopher and psychologist Fechner revived this belief in the last century. There is nothing absurd in it. But without any concessions to mythology, the imaginations of thoughtful men have been very deeply stirred by the illimitable vistas of space and time which modern science has opened out to us. Some have been most impressed by the all-pervading majesty of natural law. George Meredith in a remarkable sonnet represents Lucifer rising from his dark dominion and gazing up :

> He reached a middle height, and at the stars,
> Which are the brain of heaven, he looked, and sank.
> Around the ancient track marched, rank on rank,
> The army of unalterable law.

Wordsworth sees that the obverse of law is obedience. It is " Duty," stern daughter of the voice of God, through whom the most ancient heavens are fresh and strong ; Duty, obedience to the law of their being, which upholds all things, small and great, in their appointed courses. Others have felt only the sublimity of unlimited power displayed on so colossal a stage. Victor Hugo speaks of the arrogance of man rebuked by the spirit of earth, which itself shrinks into insignificance before the wondrous planet Saturn. Saturn pales before the Sun, the Sun before the mighty stars Sirius and Arcturus ; then the Zodiac, the Milky Way, and the vast Nebulæ that whiten the darkness, pass before his vision. Lastly, the Infinite says, " All this multiplicity lives in My sombre unity " ; and God sums up with, " I have only to breathe, and all this fades away."

Others, like George Meredith again, have been uplifted by the thought that the whole universe is compacted of the same elements, and obeys the same laws :

> So may we read, and little find them cold :
> Not frosty lamps illumining dead space,
> Not distant aliens, not senseless Powers.
> The fire is in them whereof we are born ;
> The music of their motion may be ours.
> Spirit shall deem them beckoning earth, and voiced
> Sisterly to her, in her beams rejoiced.

But others, again, have been oppressed, as Tennyson was sometimes, by the vastness of the prospect—"as this poor earth's pale history runs. What is it all but a trouble of ants in the gleam of a million million of suns?" James Thomson, the author of *The City of Dreadful Night*, finds that the thought of the universe gives a blacker hue to his pessimism:

> Necessity supreme
> With infinite mystery, abysmal dark,
> Unlighted even by the faintest spark,
> For us the flitting horrors of a dream.

And Mr. Bertrand Russell, plucking courage from despair, flings defiance, like Prometheus, against the omnipotent tyrant whom none can resist.

This feeling of awe at the vast scale on which nature works, whether it be solemn joy and consolation, as with Wordsworth, mere wonder, as with Victor Hugo, or a crushing sense of impotence, as with the writers last referred to, has been countered by some tart criticism. Do we really suppose that a star, because it is a very bulky body, must have a correspondingly large soul, or that the Creator sets more store by an enormous gas-bag than by the spirit of a saint or hero? And what does it really mean—this exhortation to worship the hypothetical Creator and sustainer of the starry heavens? Is it not the characteristic tendency of an industrial civilisation to think of everything in terms of *ownership*? Is it really a valid argument for theism to ask whether so eligible a property as the universe can possibly belong to nobody? Do we ever unconsciously argue that if we bow respectfully to a duke who owns a hundred thousand acres, we ought to pay infinitely greater respect to the largest of all landed proprietors, who possesses a million estates each a million miles in diameter, and whose title-deeds are billions of years old? Indian thought has never been impressed by this idea of ownership.

Perhaps there is a natural tendency to attach too much importance to mere bigness. The vast majority of the heavenly bodies are unfit to be the abode of conscious life, and can only illustrate, on a large scale, the laws of inorganic evolution.

But the real man of science cannot be charged with a childish love of bigness. Just now he is even more interested in the infinitely little than in the infinitely great.

Natural science is the principal vehicle of revelation to us in the twentieth century. It has modified our whole way of looking at things. The idea of evolution has transformed our outlook in dealing with almost every subject, including history, politics, and theology. The belief in uniform natural laws has banished the old notion of two orders, the natural and the supernatural, dovetailed into each other on the same plane, a notion which greatly retarded the progress of knowledge. Moreover, the scientific *temper* is as great an asset to humanity as scientific discovery. Nowhere else do we find such disinterested devotion to truth, such unquenchable faith in the power and value of disciplined intellectual labour, such bold sweeps of imagination checked by such punctiliously accurate experiments. The air breathed by science is like that of mountain heights, thin, but pure and bracing.

Science has affected both theology and morality in many ways, and must affect them much farther. After four hundred years, the Church has still failed to adapt her cosmology to the discoveries of Galileo. Officially, we clergy still have to live in a pre-Copernican universe. Otherwise, certain dogmas on which the Church insists would have no meaning. The battle against the dead hand of authority is not yet won, but the issue is certain. The educated Christian has already succeeded in fitting his creed within the framework of the universe as he knows it to be; and as the people become better educated, there will be less resistance to a reconstruction of that part of the building which is obviously crumbling. When this necessary work is done, it will be found that religion is a great gainer.

In the sphere of conduct, I will point to the greater attention to strict truthfulness, to the growing thoughtfulness for the welfare of posterity, and above all, perhaps, to the increasing recognition of our duties to our non-human fellow-creatures, which were not, as we used to be taught, created for our benefit. Our religion, philosophy, and morality have been far too anthropocentric. In the future we may even come to see truth in Aristotle's dictum, that "there are many things in the universe more divine than man," though there is great wisdom in another saying of his that nature is superhuman (*daimonia*) rather than divine (*theia*). I think it is a much-needed caution, that we have no reason to suppose that the nature of God is more fully revealed in Nature than in the mind of man. But in morality as in theology there is still very much to be done in enlightening the intelligence and the conscience of the public. The new knowledge has come quickly, and morality, like theology, is intensely conservative.

In the second half of this address I wish to speak shortly of the relation of science to religious faith. Some have thought it possible to prove the existence of God by the methods of natural science. But, in my opinion, no argument which abstracts from the religious experience can ever lead to the God of religion.

It is often said that science gives us, or tries to give us, a world of facts without values, and that this is why it excludes those aspects of reality with which religion is concerned. This is, in my opinion, a complete mistake. You cannot separate judgments of fact and judgments of value in this manner. A fact without value is no fact; a value without fact is no value. Take any branch of science you like, and you will find that it is built throughout upon a valuation of experience. Take any form of religion you like, and you will find that it is built upon what are believed to be facts. The proposed delimitation of territory will not work; it would be equally fatal to both sides.

Perhaps I ought to say a few words in justification of my statement that all science is a valuation of experience. I will not lay stress on the fact that nearly all scientific literature is steeped in valuations—that men of science habitually talk of higher and lower forms of life; that they assume that health is better than disease; that parasitism is a kind of biological sin; and that the extinction of any form of life marks it as a failure and in a sort condemns it, which means that for them existence itself is a value. These value-judgments creep into their investigations because they are men, and even if they wish to keep them out they cannot do so. But besides these, they assume, to start with, that order is better than chaos, law better than accident, correct observation and calculation better than incorrect. In so doing, they base their life's work on the values of truth, harmony, orderly succession, universal law. They hope to end by establishing that these are facts; that is their reasonable faith; but unquestionably they begin by assuming that they are values.

What we have a right to say is that the natural sciences concentrate themselves upon a certain kind of values, neglecting, for their own purposes, other kinds of values. The sciences deal almost entirely with objects which can be weighed or counted. Their standards are almost entirely quantitative. These methods are enough to ascertain the truth about certain aspects of reality, but they do not attempt to explain reality as a whole, or if they do, the attempt is a failure. Professor Eddington has lately said: "I venture to say that the division of the external world into a material world and a spiritual world is superficial, and that the deep line of cleavage is between the material and the non-material aspects of the world." The 'imponderables' are the most important things in philosophy, as Bismarck said they are in politics.

For we also know the world qualitatively. We stamp things, persons, and events as good or bad, as beautiful or ugly, judging them by ideal standards which we find within us very much as the scientist finds within him an ideal standard of truth and conformity to law. And I wish to insist earnestly—for it is the foundation on which the whole philosophy of religion is built—that these qualitative judgments are the basis of all our religious, moral, and intellectual life; that they are our deepest convictions; and that they are impartial, objective judgments of fact, no less than the judgments of natural science. Judgments of fact, I dare to say, because I repeat that a value which is no fact is no value. The affirmations of the religious consciousness claim to be eternal truths, not unrealised ideals.

This claim to objectivity by the religious consciousness is not confined to the mystics. Even Aristotle recognises the capacity of the soul for apprehending the Absolute and Eternal, though it seems to make a breach in his psychology to do so; and Spinoza, forgetting, it would seem, his doctrine of parallelism, declares that "we feel and experience that we are immortal." The late F. H. Bradley, perhaps our greatest contemporary philosopher and no friend to orthodox Christianity, says impressively: "There is nothing more real than what comes in religion. To compare facts such as these with what comes to us in outward existence would be to trifle with the subject. The man who demands a reality more solid than that of the religious consciousness knows not what he seeks."

And what does the religious consciousness affirm? In its widest sense, it affirms as living principles and universal standards of value the triple star of idealism, Goodness, Truth, and Beauty, a threefold cord not quickly broken. It affirms that these are known to us as attributes of God, and therefore the most real things that we know. Thus we are able to ascend in heart and mind to a spiritual and eternal world in which abide the thoughts of God which energise in the creation as vital laws. It is in this eternal world that we find our immortality; it is because we are not cut off from this eternal world that we know, as Spinoza says, that we are immortal.

But this is not all. The religious consciousness affirms a personal God. A personal God does not mean a magnified and non-natural man. It means a Being with whom a human person can hold personal relations. That we can hold personal relations with the Author of our being is the conviction of all religious people. Their conviction is not based on a priori reasoning; it is based on experience. Partly we think that we can trace the wise and merciful care of God in the course of our lives, the rod and the staff of His fatherly hand; but chiefly we are sure that He hears our prayers.

> Speak to Him thou, for He hears; and spirit with spirit can meet;
> Closer is He than breathing, and nearer than hands and feet.

We conclude, then, that the outstanding differences between science and religion are mainly differences of emphasis in asserting the reality of the ultimate values. The nature of our work, and of our dominant interests, leads some of us to see God in the order of nature, others in moral goodness, others in beauty, whether of nature or art. These are all divine attributes, and God manifests Himself in all three. But we have all chosen to be onesided, because only by specialising can we do any good in the world.

We none of us see all round the truth. But by the goodness of God, those who follow the gleam wholeheartedly and disinterestedly in any one direction are not much cramped by this specialising. The work to which they have given themselves takes on a universal quality, so that the beauty and goodness in the world are not hidden from those who are searching out nature's laws, and the saint feels something of the awe and wonder of the visible creation.

There is more than one path up the hill of the Lord. It is only from the top, we may say in a figure, that the paths meet and the view is the same. But true men are all engaged upon the same quest.

Cancelled from
Gladstone's Library
13 MAR 2023

THE PERSISTENT PURPOSE

THE REV. PRINCIPAL H. WHEELER ROBINSON, M.A., D.D.

Principal of Regent's Park (Baptist) College, London; President of the Baptist Historical Society; formerly Tutor in Rawdon (Baptist) College, Leeds (1906–20); *and Minister of Pitlochry Baptist Church* (1900–3), *St. Michael's Baptist Church, Coventry* (1903–6), *and South Parade Baptist Church, Headingley, Leeds* (1917–20). *He was born in Northampton in* 1872; *and after some years of business life studied at Regent's Park College, the University of Edinburgh* (1891–5), *Mansfield College, Oxford* (1895–1900), *and the University of Strassburg* (1899). *Sometime Junior and Senior Septuagint Prizeman, Houghton Syriac Prizeman, and Junior and Senior Kennicott Scholar in the University of Oxford. He has published "Deuteronomy and Joshua," in the "Century Bible," "The Christian Doctrine of Man," "The Religious Ideas of the Old Testament," "The Cross of Job," "The Cross of Jeremiah," "Baptist Principles," "The Cross of the Servant," "The Life and Faith of the Baptists," and "The Christian Experience of the Holy Spirit."*

THE PERSISTENT PURPOSE

BY THE REV. H. WHEELER ROBINSON, D.D.

"*I will not let thee go, except thou bless me.*"—Gen. xxxii. 26.

THIS is one of the many arresting sayings in which the Bible is so rich—sayings that write themselves for ever on the heart of mankind, and may become the guiding principle, the final epitome, of a human life. The saying is a paradox, for it defies reason by treating an obvious enemy as a disguised friend; but in this apparent inconsistency it ranks with other memorable paradoxes of the Bible. The helpless and agonised father, appealing to Jesus for the restoration of his son, cried, "I believe; help Thou mine unbelief." Simon Peter, at once attracted and repelled by the discovery of the unsuspected majesty of his teacher-friend, instinctively prays, "Depart from me; for I am a sinful man, O Lord." There is a paradox even on the lips of the Lord, in that perplexing cry of the Cross, which appeals to the very Father who seems to have withdrawn from His Son, "My God, My God, why hast Thou forsaken Me?"

The unforgettable cry of Jacob has a not less memorable setting. Who has not dwelt imaginatively on the familiar story of Jacob's wrestling? We think of the dark torrent rushing through the ravine, and the dangerous ford by which Jacob's company have crossed. We see this man of mingled purposes lingering behind, as though reluctant to meet again the brother he wronged so many years before. Then, in the darkness of the night, there comes the lonely struggle with the stranger, that desperate encounter for very life, the straining muscles of the locked combatants, the agonised effort, and the grim discovery by Jacob that the stranger is stronger than he. It is a defeated man who somehow penetrates to the hope of a friend behind the fact of a foe, and appeals to a hidden power and will to save and not to destroy: "I will not let thee go, except thou bless me." What is the real meaning of a story so impressive and so suggestive as this?

The early stories of a nation's origins are its unconscious art. They are not history in any scientific sense, though they may indirectly provide the materials for history. They paint a picture in words—a memorable picture, or they would not be told and retold by successive generations, long before they are written down. They are continually reshaped in their details and modified in their applications, though the nucleus of the story remains. They gather and enshrine the thoughts of one generation after another. Sometimes the beginning may be in a myth or legend far removed from the later application, for the mind of man must always have something to work on, something to assimilate and transform into its higher meanings. So it seems to be with the story of Jacob's wrestling with the stranger, in the darkness of the night by the ford of Jabbok. Perhaps it was once the story of the strife of man against nature, the struggle with the river-god who was angry with those who dared to cross his stream. At that stage it portrayed the struggle of man with the grim realities of his world, man trying to win a precarious footing against the rush of the torrent, at the peril of his life. But then it was taken up and transformed by the religion of Israel, whose God was behind and above nature. He was at first an unknown God; only by slow degrees and the ventures of faith did men come to know the wealth of compassion, the will to save and bless, which lay hidden in His heart. In that experience of Him, extending over many centuries, the essential quality of the discoverer was persistence—the will to be blessed. So we find a later prophet of Israel appealing to this very story to rebuke his own generation for their slackness: "Jacob strove with God: yea, he strove with the angel, and prevailed: he wept, and made supplication unto him. . . . Therefore turn thou to thy God: keep mercy and judgment, and wait on thy God continually."

One of the first discoveries we make in the great adventure of life is of *life's inevitabilities*. As soon as the little child begins to assert himself, he must learn that there is a world of objects round him which do not yield to his will. The hot jug on which he puts his hand, burns him; the cat he teases, scratches him; the moon for which he cries, does not come down to him from the sky. Unless he is to be that unhappy thing, a spoilt child, he will also discover a world of boys and girls, men and women, who do not always give way to him, whose wills must often assert themselves over his. When he is old enough to form his ambitions and plan his career, he is apt to forget the lessons he has learnt in other realms, and to ignore the inevitabilities of life, its stern and relentless limits, until in splendid disregard of these he bruises his shins against them. Life is a bigger and more brutal thing than we thought, and it seems strangely regardless of our own desires. We are like an artist, learning to work on some material that seems to forbid his purpose, till he has found out how to shape that purpose to the inevitabilities of his material, and make the marble yield the living form. Many a homely proverb, many a saying of the wise, teach us these stern laws of life, which reflect and continue nature's sequence of cause and effect. We learn that bad work will follow us as long as we live, that every debt we incur must sooner or later be paid, that the lost opportunity never recurs, that the past is irrevocable. We learn that unless we give we can never get (in any sense that makes things really ours), that skill must be purchased by effort and discipline, that without loving we cannot win love, or keep it when won. All these things are as necessary a part of our education as man's struggle for existence, or the child's encounter with the physical world around him. In both worlds, the world of things and the world of persons, we come to know ourselves only through knowing that which is not ourselves, that which refuses to be shaped and moulded at our mere wish. These are the realities of life, and until we learn them there is no reality in our religion. We do not really cry to God for help, we do not really pray, until we find something against which we are powerless, something from which we seek to be delivered, and from which we cannot save ourselves. The spiritual agonies through which a man must sooner or later go, if he does not drug himself by work or pleasure into unconsciousness of the real meaning of life, are the birth-hours of true and genuine religion. The ancient world saw its terrors gathered up into the forms of demons and evil spirits, and cried for deliverance from these. The modern world has brushed these forms of thought aside, but there still remains the sense of life's inevitabilities from which they sprang. There is still the handicap of some physical weakness that robs us of the prize of life when it seemed within our grasp; there is still the consciousness of the divided heart, the grip of some evil passion that will not let us go, or the scars of the old sin that will not be forgotten; there is still the great mystery of death. The proudest of us lives to learn that he is beaten and humiliated by something that is greater than himself, and unless he did learn it, he would remain an untaught fool, though all the intellectual wisdom of the ages were his.

The faith that gives the victory over these inevitabilities of life is that which sees them transformed by *God's initiatives,* that approach of God to man in and through all these things which gives to them a changed meaning. This does not mean an evasion of them, a mere flight from them. A good deal of what passes for religion is a running away from facts. These things are facts, and the only way in which their inevitability can be overcome is by changing their meaning. The Cross of Christ is the greatest example of this. In itself, it meant the inevitable end of a dreamer beating against the bars of the stern facts of life—for how could the lonely prophet of Nazareth hope to escape the cowardice, the selfishness, the prejudice, the spiritual blindness, which crucified Him? Yet the Cross of Christ was transformed by a new meaning when men saw it in the light of a victorious purpose, crowned by God, when they saw it as the measure of the world in which they lived, and of the love of God which was seeking to save that world. The Cross is a transformed inevitability. In such transformation of meaning we have the new fact, as real as the old, and more powerful. It is there we must look chiefly for God's approach, not through the chinks and crannies left between the facts, not in what has been called a piecemeal supernaturalism, but in the spiritual power to recognise God Himself under His disguise, and to call the old enemy a new friend. The old truth remains; God does not upset His laws at our whim, though all that we yet know of those laws, in nature or grace, cannot exhaust them, or limit the scope of His working. But the knowledge of His purpose to use them for our good and not for our hurt, the discovery that after all He does mean to bless and not to curse, the vision of the whole struggle of life as a necessary preparation for the fuller knowledge—all this takes the poison from the sting of death itself, and gives a present victory over life. The proof must be in the new consciousness of the life so achieved. God's greatest work is from within, rather than without, for this personal experience is the realm of His Holy Spirit. When the unbeliever tauntingly asked what God had done for Stephen, in letting him be stoned to death, the just reply was: "This is what God did for him: He gave him the power to say, 'Lord, lay not this sin to their charge.'"

The power of the Spirit of God to transform the meaning of life for us comes through God's own initiative. We love, because He first loved us. It is in and through the grace of Jesus Christ that we discover the God who has come out to meet us, sinners as we are, not in wrath but in holy love. A prophet pictures Israel's God as coming forth from Zion across the wilderness to seek His people, saying, "I have loved thee with an everlasting love; therefore with loving-kindness have I drawn thee." This is a prophecy of the parable of the Prodigal Son, and of the revelation of the Father in the Gospel and Cross of Jesus Christ. Phillips Brooks put the emphasis in the right place when he answered the question as to what had been the secret of his life by saying, "Less and less, I think, grows the consciousness of seeking God. Greater and greater grows the certainty that He is seeking us and giving Himself to us to the complete measure of our present capacity." Through the discovery of Him who has come out to meet us, we gain the new confidence that plucks victory from defeat, and share the new spirit that transforms life and life's inevitabilities. Those only are "saved" men who share the Spirit of Christ through the grace of Christ, men who no longer fear what life can do to them, because all things are theirs, and they are Christ's, and Christ is God's.

But the power of God's initiatives to transform the meaning of life's inevitabilities is conditioned by *man's persistencies*. If it is in the spirit of man that the victory has to be won, that spirit must be made God's. Now, it is our very nature that we cannot be made good or brought into fellowship with God against our desire. God's need of us cannot become effective until we are conscious of our need of Him. That is His own law—the law He has laid down in making man in His own image. But our need of Him must not be the passing wish of a moment, a sentimental longing, the base expedient of insincerity or cowardice. It must be a persistent purpose that learns to cry, out of the darkness and the apparent defeat, "I will not let thee go, except thou bless me." Try to take that as a bit of prosaic logic, and you make nonsense of it. How can man constrain God? How can man win his best victory by defeat? Yet that paradox is true of the highest and deepest things—that they pass beyond our reasonings, and prove themselves by our experience of them. It is enough that we have caught a glimpse of something beyond the appearance of things, a glimpse that comes and goes, perhaps, and leaves us desperately wondering whether we have seen anything at all—and yet a glimpse that gives us the courage and hope to go on, and teaches us to see the truth of the saying, " 'Tisn't life that matters. 'Tis the courage you bring to it."[1] There are times when a man's best wisdom, all that he has learnt from life, seems to be gathered up in two words, "Go on." We could not justify it by any argument, and yet, deep down in our hearts, we know it is the one thing to do, and we know that our manhood is tested by this one thing—our persistency in the hopeless thing for which we have once dared to hope. It may be the struggle to achieve some visible success that is worth while, some dream of our youth at which others have laughed or shrugged their shoulders. It may be the loathing of our worst selves, and the determination that no retrospect of failures, however long, shall rob us of the will to go on with the attempt. It may be for our very faith in God that we fight, as when Job cries to a God behind God, a God whose purpose is just and loving behind the God whom life's inevitabilities present as unjust and cruel. Whatever the struggle be, the one thing needful is the persistency that refuses to acknowledge defeat. It may show itself in those who seem to be hopelessly beaten, by the way in which

[1] The opening words and keynote of Hugh Walpole's novel *Fortitude*.

they cling to "some rag of honour" until the end; it may find its utterance in some last appeal from the cross to the Cross. But it is always the condition of blessing, and of the final discovery of God's will to bless, that we should ourselves persist in the struggle to win the blessing that never can be won by our own effort alone.

If these things are true—and who can deny them?—it would seem that the supreme witness that we belong to God is in our persistent purpose not to let Him go; and this is true, if we rightly understand what we are saying. It does not mean that we find assurance in our unaided effort, or even in the moral strength by which we do go on. On the contrary, it is just the fear that we shall soon let go that makes us afraid. The truth is rather that in this close and desperate grip on God we discover the yet closer grip of God on us. We shall not let Him go—because He will not let us go. He has us in His power; He has taught us our weakness; and now He will show us His strength. The proof of all this is not in any text of Scripture, though the promises of Scripture may point the way; not in any testimony of other men, though we may learn from them what and where to seek. The proof must come new and clear to our own hearts in this inner consciousness of a struggle with God Himself. We thought it was a struggle with an enemy, we find that an unknown friend is holding us. The persistency of our own purpose is, indeed, a frail and unsafe thing; but what if it is the witness of His Spirit in us, the proof of His purpose? This is where the innermost transformation of the Spirit is wrought—when He convinces us that within our wavering, despairing purpose there is God's own purpose concealed. Then we see that His grace is perfected in our weakness. We learn the truth which underlies the testimony of Israel's prophets, and indeed of all who witness for God—that ours is somehow God's, and therefore God's is ours. This is where all the great and ultimate problems of theology and philosophy are brought to a focus, in the final contact of the human spirit and the divine. With those problems, however, we are not here concerned. Our concern is with the need of the heart in all men—the need to find from life, in spite of all its constraints and sorrows, something that will make it well worth while, for ourselves and for others, something which is, in the old-fashioned phrase, "blessing." Let every one take courage to go on, for if his heart cries to God, "I will not let Thee go, except Thou bless me," it is God who utters that cry in him, and that cry is the proof that he *will* be blessed.

THE HOPE OF IMMORTALITY

THE BISHOP OF GLOUCESTER

Rt. Rev. Arthur Cayley Headlam, C.H. 1921 ; *M.A., D.D., Hon. D.D. (Aberdeen),* 1906 ; *Trinity College, Dublin,* 1926 ; *Order of St. Sava (Serbia)* 4*th Class ; born Whorlton, Durham, Aug.* 2, 1862 ; *e. s. of late Rev. A. W. Headlam ; married* 1900, *Evelyn Persis (died* 1924), *daughter of Rev. George Wingfield, Rector of Glatton, Hunts. Educated Winchester College (scholar) ; New Coll. Oxford (scholar),* 2*nd class, Class Moderations ;* 1*st class, Final Classical School ; Fellow of All Souls' College, Oxford,* 1885–97 ; *Rector of Welwyn, Herts,* 1896–1903 ; *Bampton Lecturer* 1920 ; *editor of the "Church Quarterly Review,"* 1901–21 ; *Principal of King's College, London,* 1903–12 ; *Professor of Dogmatic Theology, King's College, London,* 1903–16 ; *Regius Professor of Divinity, Oxford University, and Canon of Christ Church, Oxford,* 1918–23 ; *Some publications : joint author with Professor Sanday of a "Critical and Exegetical Commentary on the Epistle to the Romans,"* 1895 ; *"Teaching of the Russian Church,"* 1897 ; *"St. Paul and Christianity,"* 1913 ; *"The Miracles of the New Testament,"* 1914 ; *"The Doctrine of the Church and Christian Reunion" (Bampton Lectures),* 1920 ; *"The Life and Teaching of Jesus the Christ,"* 1923 ; *"The Church of England,"* 1924 ; *"Jesus Christ in Faith and History,"* 1925.

THE HOPE OF IMMORTALITY

BY THE BISHOP OF GLOUCESTER

"*And this is life eternal, that they might know Thee, the only true God.*"—John xvii. 3.

NO thoughtful person can be indifferent to the problems which this transient human life presents to us. We think of the great array of the souls of the departed, and in reverence and thoughtfulness we ask ourselves what we may know of the future. We think of our own lives and the lives of those with whom we have been associated and whom we have loved, and we ask, Is this life here the term and limit of our existence, a few years bounded on each side by eternal darkness? When we lay the body in the grave, we speak of the "sure and certain hope of the resurrection to eternal life, through our Lord Jesus Christ." What ground have we for believing in personal immortality? What can we know of the life beyond the grave? What is the end and destiny of the human race? I ask your patience for a short time to-day, while I discuss, with a feeling of humility and a consciousness of the inadequacy of anything that I can say, some of these momentous questions.

I. Let me begin with what is, I think, of some significance. The whole weight of tradition and authority is on the side of belief in some future state, that is, it has in its favour the accumulated result of the experience and reflection of the human race. In a very early period of the history of human life in the world we find, on the evidence of archæology, such a belief already existing. It is part of the teaching of almost every religion. It is held by almost every race of mankind at the present day. It has on its side the opinions of the vast majority of the great minds of every age. What is more remarkable is, I think, that although from time to time the influence of the more rationalistic, more sceptical, more materialistic thought has in this or that period or generation or sphere or circle tended to disbelief, although that belief is at times widespread, although naturally and inevitably a feeling of doubt arises among many thoughtful persons, yet the general sense of mankind has again and again rejected these negations and preserved its belief.

Now, I do not think that the testimony of authority in this as in other matters is of slight weight, for authority is, I believe, the origin and source of some of our most fundamental ideas. What is the source of our belief in that uniformity of nature which forms the major premiss of every scientific syllogism? It is that continuous and verifiable experience which is at the basis of all our authoritative beliefs. The uniformity of nature means that like causes have like effects. It is the unconscious presupposition of all our ordinary actions, and for scientific purposes becomes a formal generalisation. It tells us that the universe is a rational system and not a chaos. Now, as far as I can see, this belief comes to us simply on authority, but this authority is the result of the accumulated experience and reflection of the human race.

It is the same with regard to the fundamental postulate of all moral action, which we cannot express more simply than by saying that the good is good. This belief forms the basis of all healthy social and political life, but it is a proposition which obviously we cannot prove. Why do we believe it ? We accept it as part of the authoritative tradition of the human race. It has gradually become a settled conviction of the human mind because it is the lesson which accumulated experience has taught us. Peoples and nations have denied its truth by their practice and action and appear to us to have paid the penalty. Philosophers have attempted to analyse and explain away the good and make it a mere form of the useful or the pleasant, but they have never ultimately secured assent. All experience seems to corroborate our inherited belief in righteousness as an integral and fundamental element in the structure of human life.

So it is, I believe, with the belief in a future life in some form or other, with the doctrine of the immortality of the soul. It has become part of the authoritative tradition of human life, and is accepted by most men on that authority, not without reflection, but for the most part without demanding logical proof. That is not in itself a condemnation, for, as we have seen, it is the basis of acceptance of the most fundamental postulates of science and social life. These are accepted by most people on the basis of authority, and that is sufficient evidence for all our common beliefs unless new experience and discovery prove their untruth. For this authority means a continuous spiritual experience. We shall attempt shortly to analyse that experience and estimate its value. The point we have now to make is that this experience goes back to a very early period in the history of the human race and has been continuous and almost universal. The postulates of religion, as of science and of all other departments of human thought and life, are all alike part of the authoritative tradition of the race.

No doubt authority is not infallible. Each generation receives beliefs, customs, and rules of life as part of this tradition, which experience shows it must discard or modify. An imperfect experience has to give way to something which is found to be more correct. An inherited belief which cannot be realised in experience passes away. There must be a process of correction as well as of tradition. But, as regards most fundamental beliefs, the process of the development of the human mind has been rather to strengthen than to weaken them, and they have been gradually transformed from half-understood convictions into philosophical principles. That is the case, for example, with the uniformity of nature or the fundamental postulates of morality. So it is, I believe, with the belief in immortality. In the earliest ages of the human race it was something very crude and materialistic; it has become, under the influence of philosophical reflection and divine revelation, a lofty and inspiring doctrine.

I have noted recently two curious accusations brought against religious beliefs by scientific writers. They point out how crude were religious beliefs in their origin, and how the variations of religious belief are so great that no one can say what is true. It is implied, of course, that in the case of science things are different.

Now, I do not think that there is any justification for that attitude. Turn to the origins of science. We find the beginnings of our scientific knowledge just as crude and just as absurd (from our modern point of view) as any primitive religious beliefs. Of course we must realise that in relation to their own time they are not absurd. They only become so when preserved to the present day, and compared with present-day beliefs. There has been development in religion. There has been to an equal extent development in science. Many uninstructed people at the present day hold crude religious views, but it is also true that outside the limited circle of adepts there is no form of scientific absurdity which is not capable of being accepted. More than that, it is probable that in a short time most of the scientific ideas of the present day will be looked upon as inadequate or absurd. I notice that this year a considerable part of the address of the President of the British Association was devoted to criticising somewhat caustically the address delivered at a meeting held at Leeds sixty-nine years ago by Professor Owen, the leading biologist of that day. Both addresses appear to me to be somewhat over-dogmatic in their assertions, and somewhat precarious in their arguments, and I could not but wonder whether sixty-nine years hence another address might not be delivered on the same subject criticising the opinions of the present day equally caustically. Religion and science alike should be judged by their highest attainments, and the primitive superstitions of savages are no more valuable as an argument against religion than the curious conceptions of early scientists are an argument against the attainments of the scientific world of the present day.

Nor can science make any greater claim to unanimity than religion. At the present moment there is the greatest variation of opinion concerning Evolution. The Newtonian theory of gravitation appears to be in process of being superseded. Each successive generation of scientific men condemns, often with some scorn, the imperfect attainments of its predecessors, and forgets that future generations will be equally ready to criticise the imperfect generalisations which are in vogue at the present day. I find that the science that I was taught authoritatively fifty years ago is wrong or imperfect. There is no finality or infallibility or unanimity in scientific things. What, then, are we to say of religion ?

It is undoubtedly true that in religion there is much controversy, that both in the expression of religious truth and on questions of Church order there is much variety, and that on a vast number of points the differences of opinion between Christians are great. But if I turn to the fundamental truths of the Christian faith, I find a remarkable agreement. God, the revelation of God in Jesus Christ, the inspiration of mankind by the Holy Spirit, the power of the atoning death of Christ, the principles of Christian morality, duty, righteousness, service, love, sacrifice, the belief in judgment and immortality—on all these points there is no hesitation or doubt in any Christian Church at the present day. There is great variety in theological explanation, but East and West, Roman and Orthodox, Catholic and Protestant, all agree in these fundamental truths. And what is true in this age is true of all the ages. There is no difference in the fundamental truths which Ignatius taught in the second century, or Athanasius in the fourth, or Aquinas in the thirteenth, or Luther in the sixteenth, or Newman in the nineteenth. The agreed authority of the Christian Church is one of the most impressive facts in human life.

I do not know that any more impressive instance of

this could be given than the recent conference on Faith and Order held at Lausanne in August of this year. At that Conference many points of disagreement were discussed with great frankness, but a statement of belief in the Gospel of Christ was drawn up and received with complete unanimity, and in this the essential truth of the Christian faith is put forward with sincerity, with conviction, and with power. No one who reads it can doubt the essential religious unity of the Christian Church.

II. We have received, then, on the basis of widespread authority, the belief in immortality as one of the fundamental postulates of religion, and we find that it has the same authority as the postulates of science and of our moral and social life. What, then, are the grounds of this widespread belief?

First, there is the ultimate reality of the spiritual. Here we have the great issue. The material facts of the universe appear, at any rate at first sight, to be clear, definite, and certain. These we know. Is there any reason for thinking that there is anything else? Undoubtedly we know life as an attribute of our material body. Is there any reason why we should think that it can exist apart from that body? All our conscious life acts through material agents: is there any reason for looking at it as more than a temporary characteristic of certain material particles? When they vanish, it vanishes. So from time to time theories have been evolved, hypothetical constructions of the origin of the universe and human life, deriving all things from a purely material source, explaining all life and human intelligence and activity in terms of matter, accounting for the world on purely mechanistic principles and the working of chance. Such a scheme of things we know in its most superb form in the great poem of Lucretius, and some, although I think not many, modern men of science have thought that they have found a justification for such a scheme in those modern theories of development which we call for convenience "Evolution." Whatever justification such schemes may have, they harmonise with the crude, materialistic facts of life, and are accepted by those who can see nothing outside the limit of their senses.

Now, you will not expect me within the short space of an hour to deal with these theories with any degree of completeness. I can only touch on the heads of the argument, and estimate their value. Let me begin with the appeal that is made not to argument, but to the imagination, or, as I should be inclined to put it, to a limited or defective imagination. The apparent strength of the argument for materialism is held to lie in what is considered to be the argument from common sense. Let us stick to what is real. There are the things which I can touch and taste and see—they are real—anything else is merely a matter of conjecture or of imagination or of fancy. Let us stick, then, to what we know exists and not trouble about anything more, and let us take care that we get a full enjoyment of material things and of this life.

But are these things so real? and is this common sense? Is the material world which undoubtedly presses upon our senses with such urgency really the cause of all things? Can we conceive the wonderful order and beauty of the world arising purely by chance and accident without any rational cause? Are the ideals and aspirations, the intellectual achievements, the emotions and passions, the spiritual longings of mankind, but the many-coloured foam on the surface of a material sea? Neither the ordinary sense of mankind nor philosophic thought has been able to accept this as true. Human reason revolts against a non-rational origin of things. If it is hard for the human mind to conceive or understand God, it is still harder for it to understand how the non-rational could produce the rational. No materialistic explanation of the world has ever received ultimate acceptance. It is not an adequate hypothesis.

Let me try to put the argument scientifically. It must be recognised that we cannot demonstrate logically or prove the reality and existence of the things that transcend experience as we can prove a proposition in Euclid. What we are able to do is to analyse experience and to ask what explanation of experience is adequate. Our experience is twofold. It is an experience of the world and an experience of ourselves. Now, our experience of the world inevitably leads us to a mind and reason which is the ultimate cause of things. It is not possible (as is being realised more and more) to eliminate the idea of purpose from the universe. There is no alternative between chance and purpose, and the attempt to explain the development of life by mechanical laws has not been found adequate. We can, within certain limits at any rate, explain the mechanism by which things work, but that does not explain how they have come to be what they are any more than the course of a motor-car can be explained by its mechanism without reference to a driver. So strongly is this felt that for the word "Evolution" such phrases as "Creative Evolution" or "Emergent Evolution" are substituted, but they do not offer any real explanation.

How did it come to be that things should exist such as to come to be what they are? How has it been possible that variations should arise and development take place in such a way to produce an end? The idea of the end must be present before the development has begun. If that be the case, it must already exist, and I do not see how an idea can exist except in a mind. The evidence for reason and purpose cannot be eliminated, and reason and purpose can only exist in a person. Pantheism is really a mere phrase. It is only a more subtle form of materialism. We know reason and purpose only as an attribute of mind. If therefore we discover evidence of their existence, there must be mind, and mind implies person. The ultimate constitution of things leads us to a personal God.

And the testimony of the experience that we have of ourselves leads us in the same direction. Our experience of life tells us that ultimately the real and abiding things of the world are not our material environment, which will certainly pass away, but the spiritual values of life —truth and beauty, righteousness and love. We have to explain and account for man's intellectual equipment, the fact of his self-consciousness, and what in the philosophical phraseology in fashion at the moment are called values, his capacity of forming judgments of value, and their correspondence with the realities of life. In other words, we have to explain man as an intelligent moral being, with a capacity for investigating and in some way attaining a knowledge of the world of which he is a part, capable of being himself, as he believes, an efficient cause of things, of forming ideals of righteousness and beauty, and of living and acting in accordance with those ideals. All this leads us to the conception of man as a spiritual being, whose origin and essence consists not in his material framework—which is no doubt derived from an animal ancestry—but in his spiritual nature, according to which he is made in the image of God. And as our study of human nature leads us to the conviction of the reality of man's spiritual nature, so it corroborates our belief in the existence of a personal God. For it tells us that the world is a world of values and not of material things, and that these values—truth, righteousness, beauty, love, sacrifice—have no reality except in relation to a person.

Now, if our analysis is right and the ultimately real thing is the spiritual represented to us by God and the human soul, two deductions follow: one relating to God, the other to human life.

If there be a God in personal relationship with man, we find it difficult to think of Him as condemning to annihilation those spiritual beings that have lived for His service. Let me quote the words of one of the most profound of modern philosophers:

God Himself [says Professor Pringle Patterson] is at once the supreme Reality, and as Dante calls him, the supreme value—"il primo, il summo Valore." And the highest conception we can form of perfect personality is Love, not in any shallow sentimental sense, but the self-giving Love which expends itself for others, and lives in all their joys and sorrows. Such love, then, the principle of our argument bids us take as the ultimate value of which the universe is the manifestation. It bids us conceive the inmost being of God not solely as the realisation of eternal Truth and the enjoyment of perfect Beauty, but pre-eminently as the exercise and fruition of His nature as Love. And if so, the value of the finite world to the Spirit of the universe must lie, above all else, if one may so speak with modesty and reverence, in the spirits to whom He has given the capacity to make themselves in His own image. The spirits themselves must be the values to God, not simply the degrees of intelligence and virtues abstractly considered, which they respectively realise. They are not made, then—we seem justified in concluding—to be broken up and cast aside and to be replaced by relays of others in a continual succession.[1]

And the second deduction from this belief in the spiritual nature of reality is concerned with human life and the nature and purpose of humanity.

Our knowledge of the material universe tells us that it is rational, that it attains what appears to be its aim and purpose, and that there is no futility in it. We may reasonably believe that human life must be equally rational. Now, man has certain moral principles, a continuous urge to righteousness, a conscience which does not allow him to be content with neglecting the imperious demands of the moral law. If he disobeys this conscience he is not fulfilling what on the principles which we have discussed, is his purpose and destiny. But if he obeys, if he responds to his higher nature, it may well be that for him the result will be suffering, sorrow, and death. Now, if this death be the end of human life, the world is both unjust and irrational. Man is given lofty and high ideals, and he follows them, and the only result for him is failure. A world so made would be unjust, and the continuous failure of all men to attain the end for which they were created implies that human life is a futile chaos. And the result is an impossible contrast between a material world where reason seems

[1] *The Idea of Immortality*, by A. Seth Pringle-Pattison, pp. 190, 191.

to hold sway and a human world which is vain. The literature of scepticism and unbelief always seems to me to present to us a vain and futile world. But if this life be a time of probation for something higher, then human morality and the purpose of the world find their justification. This argument does not mean simply that in return for a certain amount of misery here we obtain rewards hereafter—that is a caricature of the argument—but rather that the purpose and aim with which mankind was created can in the end be attained.

The reality of the moral facts of the world leads inevitably to the two ideas of judgment and immortality. The reality of God, the relation of God to man, spiritual values, need of judgment, these are the fundamental facts on which the human mind has pondered for generations, and which have found their expression in the belief in immortality.

III. So far we have been investigating our subject from the point of view of what is sometimes, rather curiously I think, called natural religion. But to us as Christians the belief in immortality comes as part of the Christian Revelation, and the authority of Christianity turns what might be only a philosophical hypothesis into a religious conviction. We turn, then, to the Revelation which comes in Christ, and we begin with the preparation for that Revelation in the Old Testament.

It is a remarkable and perhaps a significant fact, that in comparison with some of the surrounding nations, and in particular with the Egyptians, the Hebrews had but a very dim belief in any future state. The doctrine of Sheol contrasts in a most remarkable way with the elaborate ceremonial, magical, and ethical development of the Book of the Dead. The religion of Israel was in its essence a religion for this world. It taught us of righteousness and judgment and of a God whose providential love ruled the world, and it grasped fully the power of righteousness as a force in human life and the earthly value of a good life. But gradually the limitations of such a creed became apparent. The older belief ultimately developed into the prudent worldliness of the Book of Ecclesiasticus. It was comparatively easy to believe that to fulfil the law—moral and ceremonial—was the right way to obtain a comfortable and successful life, if you lived at Jerusalem during the peaceful and tolerant rule of the Ptolemies and were a member of the governing class. The temple aristocracy ruled the city. Its wealth was derived from religious sources, and every motive of prudence and interest taught you that the basis of commercial success and a prosperous career depended on loyalty to the established religion. But a great change was to come.

The preparations were laid in the movements of religious thought and in the sincerity of religious life. The development of the idea of God made the conception of Sheol—a place without God—impossible. The pious temple worshipper who had little in common with the temple aristocracy felt that the ultimate reality was life in the presence of God. He did not take such a complacent view of worldly success. He saw the ungodly in great prosperity. The author of the book of Job had a far more profound insight into human nature, even than the author of Ecclesiasticus. The problems were not so easy as the Son of Sirach had thought. Moreover, there was a new conception of the worth of the individual. As the Jew became denationalised he could not think only of the future of the Israelite community, and What would happen if the salvation of Israel meant the death of the Israelite?

And then the awakening came. The Seleucidæ took the place of the Ptolemies. Antiochus Epiphanes became the champion of the gods of Hellas, and instead of religious peace came persecution. The temple aristocracy failed. They were quite ready to conform to the new order of things, and the higher religion of the world was only saved by the piety of the Chasidim and the heroism of the Maccabees. But how inadequate the limitations of the older religion appear to be! If the fulfilment of the will of God and the life in the presence of God were the only things worth living for, how could we account for the fact that it was just those who obeyed God's will who were cut off from life? And did that mean that they were cut off for ever from the presence of the God for whom they lived and for whom they sacrificed everything? Clearly that was impossible. They might lose everything, but they could not lose God, and so the culmination came to the teaching of Israel on the destiny of man:

The souls of the righteous are in the hand of God,
And no torment shall touch them.
In the sight of the foolish they seemed to have died:
And their departure was counted to be their hurt,
And their journeying away from us to be their ruin:
But they are in peace.
For even if in the sight of men they be punished,
Their hope is full of immortality:
And having borne a little chastening, they shall receive great good:
Because God made trial of them and found them worthy of Himself.
As gold in the furnace He proved them,
And as a whole burnt offering He accepted them,

> And in their time of visitation they shall shine forth,
> And as sparks among stubble they shall run to and fro.
> They shall judge nations, and have dominion over peoples :
> And the Lord shall reign over them for evermore.
> They that trust in Him shall understand truth :
> And the faithful shall abide with Him in love :
> Because grace and mercy are to His chosen.

IV. The doctrine of immortality which was the final attainment of the religion of Israel was completed and established through the revelation in Christ. The evidence of Christianity is twofold. There is, first of all, the evidence of the Resurrection of Christ, and then connected indeed with it but wider in its appeal the witness of Christianity to the power and reality of the spiritual.

Now, I do not wish to dwell to-day at any length on the first of these. It is naturally something which demands a special investigation. That I have attempted, however imperfectly, to make elsewhere. What I do wish to say is that I think that the tendency in some circles is to underrate the importance of this evidence. There is a shrinking from the appeal to history. The evidence for spiritual truth is to be found only in experience. Now, I believe that experience alone is a most unsubstantial basis, because experience is very largely itself the result of teaching and environment. What is true of experience is that in it we have the verification of the truth of our doctrines. But it does not give us either the source or the evidence.

The source and the evidence come from an historical revelation, and are stronger, I would hold, than is sometimes suggested at the present day. It is not only that the authenticity and, within certain limits, the historical value of the documents have been more firmly established. I think no one acquainted with the facts would doubt that. But there is also the failure to provide any adequate hypothesis to account for the facts. The evidence, for example, for the empty tomb is historically good. It is disbelieved by some really because it seems to them inconsistent with what they believe about the nature and character of the Resurrection. But read any of the theories put forward to account for the story, and their futility will be apparent. They rarely satisfy many except those who invent them.

And the narrative as we have it explains rationally and intelligently the existence of Christianity. There can be no doubt that the Crucifixion and the apparent failure of our Lord's life had for the moment shattered the faith of the Apostles. There is no doubt that some event happened which completely transformed them from hesitating, doubting, feeble followers into ardent preachers of the Gospel. There is no doubt as to the reason of this change. It was the convinced and sincere belief in the Resurrection, and for that belief they gave a coherent and adequate account. They had found the tomb empty and, under circumstances which had impressed them by their reality, the risen Lord had appeared to them. The whole narrative is self-consistent. We know that it is early. We know that theories of imposture are not tenable, and we have in it an adequate cause for the greatest spiritual fact in the history of mankind. I do not think that we should lightly reject such evidence.

But now I want to turn to the wider evidence that Christianity gives for the truth of the Resurrection. Christianity is the greatest illustration of the power and reality of spiritual forces. It is founded entirely on spiritual beliefs; it has grown through the power of those beliefs. When its methods have been spiritual, it has flourished. When it has appealed to material resources, to the power of the sword, to the authority of the State, or to the influence of wealth, it has become corrupt. While the kingdoms of this world have passed away, it has grown continually and it is still growing. It has created all that is most permanent in our modern civilisation, and there are many who believe that that civilisation cannot stand except on a Christian basis. Now, this great spiritual force is built on the belief in the Resurrection. There has never been any doubt as to the basis of its claims and the character of its teaching.

Now, what does this imply? Does it not suggest that it is the spiritual phenomena which harmonise with the realities of the world? It is natural for us, at first sight, to think that the strongest things are the material. A great empire built up on material power, wealth, armaments, widely extended possessions, appears to be something very strong and lasting. But we know that there is nothing so transitory, and we know that it is spiritual influences, and not merely material strength, that are necessary to give stability to an empire or kingdom. This alone proves to us, I think, the reality of the spiritual. And then we turn to the Christian Church, and we find that it has a power and vitality which contrast remarkably with the transiency of world empires. Are we not reasonable in holding that this power of survival means that its teaching is adapted to human life and therefore true? How unsubstantial and powerless the Christian society seems compared with the strength of the material society. Yet it continues to survive, even although exposed to the most brutal attacks. Does not this attest its reality? I can well believe in the survival of a society based on what is true but imperfect; I cannot believe that what is based on the fundamentally false should persist for nearly two thousand years. The point that I would emphasise is that Christianity is by far the greatest spiritual force in the world, that its history, its work, and its life tell us of the reality and power of the spiritual, and that it is built on the belief in personal immortality and therefore testifies to the truth. It is the appeal for the verification of our beliefs to the accumulated experience of mankind.

V. We believe the future life, then, because we believe in the reality of the spiritual, because we believe that fundamentally the world is a world of spiritual values and not of material forces, because of the witness of Christianity. The grounds of our belief will tell us all that we can know of the life to come.

It has always been the custom of the Christian as of other religions to express its hope in symbolical forms. The human mind, especially the uneducated mind, naturally demands something concrete. It is only the educated man that can realise abstract ideas. So at the time when the belief in a future life first impressed itself on the mind of Israel, there sprung up a considerable literature seeking to give concrete and accurate expression to these new ideas. An elaborate cosmology and an elaborate eschatology were constructed. Their source was partly perhaps eastern religions, partly the religious imagination. A considerable phraseology was provided and the future abode of the human race was mapped out with great precision. This became the natural language for the expression of religious ideas, and as such was taken over in the New Testament. Yet it is important to notice how little of it was taken over, and how simple are the ideas of the New Testament, compared, for example, with the book of Enoch. But Christian literature took over much that the New Testament had left out, and in the Middle Ages this heritage was combined with the great picture of the future life which Roman paganism had given us in Vergil, to produce (as its best known and greatest exposition) the vision of Dante. All these pictures and symbols helped the religious life of the Middle Ages, but whether or no they were always taken literally we cannot say. It is always difficult to know how far a poet believes in his own creations. But they became the basis of an over-elaborate dogmatic construction, and to many at the present day they present a burden rather than an assistance.

There is always the danger of over-literalness, but I do not think there is any justification for this. Let us turn back to the New Testament. Our Lord uses naturally the religious phraseology of His own time; this we know to have been the characteristic of His teaching in all directions, and nothing else would have been possible. But in this way He teaches us the two fundamental ideas of Judgment and Union with God, and these represent the truths which lie at the basis of the Christian belief in a future state. God judges. Man deserves and needs judgment. The injustice and imperfection of the present world can only be corrected in and through the Divine judgment. That is clearly taught us by our Lord Himself, and throughout the New Testament; but the pictures which have been created of the Last Judgment need not be taken as a literal representation of what will be.

" But when the Son of Man shall come in His glory, and all the angels with Him, then shall He sit on the throne of His glory : and before Him shall be gathered all the nations ; and He shall separate them one from another, as the shepherd separateth the sheep from the goats : and He shall set the sheep on His right hand, but the goats on the left. Then shall the King say unto them on His right hand, Come, ye blessed of My Father, inherit the kingdom prepared for you from the foundation of the world : for I was an hungred, and ye gave Me meat : I was thirsty, and ye gave Me drink : I was a stranger, and ye took Me in ; naked, and ye clothed Me : I was sick, and ye visited Me : I was in prison, and ye came unto Me " . . . and then the explanation, " Inasmuch as ye did it unto one of the least of these My brethren, ye did it unto Me."

Now, the ethical and spiritual value of this parable is unequalled, but are we to take it in its literal signification, and suppose that it is an exact picture of what is going to happen ? Surely not. We do not interpret other parables in that way, nor should we do so in this case. The very fact that our Lord speaks of " sheep and goats " is, I think, significant.

The parable tells us of the reality and conditions of judgment, but neither here nor in other cases need we give a literal interpretation to the eschatological language which was part of the current theological phraseology.

There is one more point which must be considered. We believe in God, and in God's judgment of mankind —how and in what way we need not trouble to ask. But does this commit us to those harsh descriptions of

Divine judgment which some have constructed ? Surely not. For they are drawn from a partial study of the Scriptures and are inconsistent with what we are told of the Divine mercy : " God willeth that all men should be saved and come to the knowledge of the truth." But the real answer is that (our fundamental proposition is that) God is righteous, and that therefore the judgment, whatever it may be, will be certainly just. Nor am I troubled by the metaphysical objections that it is not possible to ascribe the quality of righteousness or justice to the absolute, for the God of religion is not apprehended by our logical faculties.

" And so we shall be ever with the Lord " ; " This is life eternal, to know Thee, the only God." Here is the sum of what the Christian believes. It means that the future life is a continuance of all that is highest and best in our life here. The soldier who voluntarily gives up his life for the sake of his comrades or his cause will reach a moral height which few of us can attain. I remember reading a letter written by a quite commonplace young fellow on the eve of a great offensive in which he was killed. It revealed to me the human soul. Everyone has his moments of lofty affections, of deep religious emotions, of heroic effort, of glowing aspiration, and he knows that they are the greatest moments of his life.

It is thus that even here he can be with God, and it is these that are the foretaste of the life with God to come.

For Christianity teaches us that life—eternal life—is something that may begin here, and is continued hereafter. We may picture this eternal life in any shape we will. That is merely to translate into symbolical language transcendental truths. The reality of that language lies in the reality of Divine judgment and the fulfilment of the destiny of the human soul in an eternal union with God.

And let no one question these things because our imagination fails to grasp their possibility. It is to the rational mind a failure of imagination which is the great cause of difficulty in believing in human immortality. But science has gradually revealed to us a world of infinite possibilities. The old material heaven and hell cannot be as they were once believed to be. But all that we have learnt of the vast expansion of the universe in space, or the subtle constitution of things, or the wonders of life, or the potentialities of mind, opens before us the thought that there is nothing too high or too lofty for us to believe and conceive; and in a universe so wonderfully constituted, in a universe the spiritual springs of which we can know so little, in a universe where the fundamental ideas of space and time vanish in the analysis of the human mind, there need be no limit to the religious aspirations which reason justifies.

A FRIEND OF PUBLICANS AND SINNERS

THE REV. PHILIP NAPIER WAGGETT, S.S.J.E., D.D.

The Rev. Philip Napier Waggett, now Vicar of University Church in Cambridge, is the second son of John Waggett and Florence Blechynden Waggett. He was educated at Charterhouse, and Christ Church, Oxford. Interested first in classics and then in biological science, in which he took a first class at Oxford. M.A. Oxford and Cambridge (Trinity College). In the early days of school and college missions he was at the Christ Church Mission in Poplar, and later at the Charterhouse Mission in Southwark, and he was lately for eight months at the latter mission. In the interval, as a Priest of the Society of St. John the Evangelist, he has lived in South Africa, America, Oxford, Cambridge, and Westminster. During the War he was first a Chaplain in France, 1914–17, *being twice mentioned in dispatches, and later engaged as a Political Officer on the Headquarters' Staff in Palestine. He went to India on the Mission of Help, and was most of last year at the General Theological Seminary of the Episcopal Church of America, New York. Select Preacher at Oxford and at Cambridge. Among his writings are: "Science and Religion," "The Scientific Temper in Religion," "Knowledge and Virtue" (Hulsean Lectures: Clarendon Press), "The Industry of Faith." He is a Proctor in Convocation for the Clergy of the Diocese of Oxford.*

A FRIEND OF PUBLICANS AND SINNERS [1]

BY THE REV. PHILIP NAPIER WAGGETT, D.D.

"*A friend of publicans and sinners.*"—Matt. xi. 19.

I. THE gentleness of Christ is even better known than the "sweet reasonableness" celebrated by Matthew Arnold. Gentleness, indulgence, an unmitigated tolerance and all-embracing welcome of the faulty as of the weak, a tenderness that admits no touch of scorn or harshness or resentment, a homely, unsuspecting friendliness that shrinks from no companionship and makes Him sit with excommunicated worldlings and broken or prosperous outcasts: these are the well-known and ever-welcome qualities of the Divine, most human Saviour.

He is meek and lowly of heart. He went about doing good to all. The poor He favours and the rich He does not exclude. There is in Him, we say, no assertion of superior virtue, no recoil from sinful or shameful persons. The often guilty rich man shall be His host; the scandalous are qualified for His table. His spiritual perception and moral sensitiveness are made suspect by this uncritical humanity. A real prophet, those who watched Him said, would know the identity and the character of people who touched Him. Where is His clairvoyance, where is His "gift"? It would seem He carries no Ithuriel spear. The disreputable pass easily the untesting test of His compassion, to the reward

[1] Preached before the Judge of Assize at Cambridge.

of His companionship. What excited the scorn of the godly in His time constitutes throughout the world to-day the warrant for our reverence, so that we should love to see over every altar and every Church porch the words "This man receiveth sinners, and eateth with them."

2. We who have been ever so little instructed in His school recognise in such appreciation as I have just imagined some omissions, some unbalanced statements; but no shafts of gratitude are aimed quite amiss. We know there was in Him a full knowledge of mankind, the frank claim of sinlessness; that His words, His silence, His presence could be a terror to the self-seeking and the self-righteous.

But we do well not to modify or moderate our impression of His tenderness and compassion. For His mercy and pity are unqualified and unlimited.

He allows and accepts all. His method of reform for a treacherous companion is the method of persevering and repeated pardon. We are tempted to say that, in His court, inconsistency and inconstancy are favoured.

It is not true that His mind is neutral or His choice without differentiation. There are prizes and blanks in His world too. There is a pearl of great price for which prudence itself will give all other possessions; there is a life for which the world is well lost.

But when persons are in the scales, His values seem almost the reverse of ours. It is not for the best in our judgment, but for the worst that He seeks. He came to call not the morally accomplished, but the morally insignificant—not the righteous, but the sinners. Sin is a fall; the sinner is in a pit; and it is just he who must be recovered, like a valuable beast—even on the Sabbath day.

The criminal is "a casualty," and commands by his moral disaster all the resources of a heaven-sent physician. It would seem that He did not turn aside from the sinner to secure any of the best of men; and in the foundation of His system it is not the noblest mind and strongest character that must be recruited at the cost of a hundred laggards and a hundred deserters, as in Gideon's enterprise; it is precisely the deserter himself who must be found, at the risk, it would seem to us, of losing the steadfast; it is the traitor who must be recalled to the standard and entrusted with the watchword.

We are tempted to say that if He discriminates, He discriminates in favour of the undeserving.

In the last dread crisis, when He accomplishes His exodus at Jerusalem, there are men who accuse and judge, who mock and scourge and crucify Him; there are men who insult Him in His hour of death, and blaspheme and would add bitterness to what seems His helpless, friendless end. For these, upon His throne of sacrifice, He presents to His Father the assured demand of the coequal Son, not for punishment, but for pardon. A robber justly suffering by His side is chosen to be the companion of His heavenly rest. *This* man shall come—unprepared, swarthy from the suns of sin—shall come, with no title but his known need and the compassion of Jesus, to the Paradise of God. It is a compassion not uncostly or uncalculating, but unlimited, unrelenting. He bore the sin of many; being reviled He reviled not again, but bore our sins in His own body on the Cross. By His *stripes* we are healed.

3. And the preferences of Christ are the preferences of Heaven itself. "Up there," in the sphere of reality and clear truth, there is more joy among the angels

over one sinner whose heart is changed than over ranks of just persons who need no change of heart. One coin in a hoard is distinguished by nothing but this—it is missing. And this is the coin to seek and find; of this the recovery is celebrated. There is a sheep in a flock, prized above the rest only because it is a strayer and does not answer to the owner's voice. It is found and becomes a prize. This lost one is worth a descent from heaven to earth; worthlessly worth a descent from earth to hell. Christ, who tells us of it, is the Good Shepherd and giveth His life for the sheep. The supreme Righteousness, God Himself, Father, Son, and Holy Spirit, is pictured not obscurely in the Parable of the Wayward Son as pouring special gifts of love upon the ungrateful soul; and what soul, conscious of its own graceless perversity, but can bear witness to this amazing more-than-miracle of favour? There are two sons, but one is made a hero of the story and of the home. He is headstrong and selfish. He demands his patrimony in haste, and without delay exiles himself to luxury, to servitude, and to starvation. Humbled or prudent, he returns; and before he can finish his plea for hired service, the father in the story falls on his neck, and with hurried commands accumulates upon this one the tokens of welcome. There is another son, a home-keeper, diligent and obedient, who has worked harder than any hired servant and has demanded no indulgence. Without waiting for his return from the farm, the feast must begin and the music strike up; and to the banquet it is the self-estranged who must be ushered as the welcome guest, the robe of honour on his servile shoulders, the ring of state on his dishonoured hand. It is he who is distinguished. He carries the magic of a bitter and once hopeless regret; he has, in the father's love, the wonder and the light of a resurrection from the grave. "This my son was dead, and is alive again; he was lost, and is found."

4. This is our earliest lesson of the spirit of Christ, the spirit of God. It is a spirit of unregarding welcome, finding guests in the alleys and squares of the city, the roads and hedges of the country. Only our Saviour's own words can suggest His tolerance. We do well to take the lesson first, and without mixing our water with its wine. And this for two reasons. First, it best fits our state as transgressors; and secondly, it is a temper most welcome to our deeper humanity when it is displayed, but least natural to our temperament and habit till we are called to ourselves.

We are not born tolerant. All of us are born judges. In the nursery, many start in life generous and even gentle; but few start uncritical and undiscriminating. It is only under the discipline of many years' experience of our own mistakes that we begin to be tolerant; only in rare hours or moments of insight and openness to the Spirit of God that we share in some small measure the love that overcomes evil with good. Only in that hour of fuller life do we find that integrity and kindness are one, that mercy and truth have met together. There is no part of our lives that can be spared from the watchful cultivation of patience, gentleness, generosity, if we are to die less un-Christlike than we were born.

We may indeed recognise with deep thankfulness the influence of this Divine example even in regions of human life that seem little conscious of the call of faith. Everywhere and in all kinds of people this tenderness

ST. DEINIOL'S
HAWARDEN
LIBRARY

of Christ spreads like a leaven. It has become a steady element in the world. In the cold oceans of rivalry, the icy seas of resentment, it is warm streams bearing fruitful life.

We are not concerned to say that mercy is peculiar to Christianity, for we know that the Eternal Word, keeping and haunting His own world, has left Himself in no age or society without a witness. But we recognise that the secret of the few has, under the influence of the Word Incarnate, become the sunlight of many, and our hearts are moved with gratitude to Him and with delight in those who have learned to pity and to pardon. Our Lord's conception of pardon was new even to men trained within hearing of the old Bible with all its teaching of the divine pardon.[1]

St. Peter's question, "How oft shall I forgive?" indicates a conception nearer to a justified acquittal than to an unlimited forgiveness—nearer to the idea practically obeyed by Christians who recognise some persons and actions as forgivable.

II. Were the critics of our Lord justified? Is it true that the Friend of sinners proved, against His own intention, the encourager of sinners in sin? Supposing the Pharisees gifted with powers of prophecy, might they have said that the new principle of pardon was to be realised by the least strictly social members of the society He was to substitute for the ruined Temple of frankly retributive Law?

[1] ἄφεσις and ἀφίημι are not, I believe, found in ancient literature in their Bible sense of forgiveness or remission of sin. The words have been adopted in the New Testament to represent the idea of pardon already prominent in the Old.

What, then, are we to say of the whole system of our social discipline? "The punishment of wickedness and vice," that protection of the weak which involves of necessity the restraint of the violent and the malicious? Or, again, of the whole department of human justice, the class of men devoted to the detection of deceit and the exposure of the fraudulent—an exposure which must to certain natures be more terrible than the sentence of death? And when we consider our national system of justice, we know that it is on the one hand but the model on a larger scale of the discipline of every smaller society—a university, a school—and, on the other hand, finds an analogue in national defence and in the fulfilment of duties in the international sphere by force. What are we to make of this?

Before we attempt any answer, let us at once confess that we are immeasurably restrained from following the example or from obeying the precept of Christ, for both the example and the precept are absolute. An answer to these difficulties is easy enough for those who admire Christ as one among many teachers, and who would sweeten the cup of their thought and of their conduct by an ingredient drawn from His life, an ingredient of unmixed mercy and tenderness. Such men often add to their partial, moderate acceptance of this example the declaration that historical Christianity has nothing whatever to do with Christ. The case is different for us who accept Him as Master and Lord. We also acknowledge that our Christianity is very far from Him; that we have never really had faith to try the experiment of forgiveness and cannot tell what magic it would disclose were we ever thoroughly to give it trial. But to despair is not enough, and there is something in us that recognises and honours the efforts of justice and even of punishment.

Shall we say that in the department of discipline we simply leave aside the example of Jesus Christ ? He is our comforter in trouble, but we must find another leader for the most difficult parts of our duty ?

Or shall we find consolation in supposing that Christ, who was once simply our friend, will make a different manifestation of Himself when He comes again to be our Judge, that the consoler of sinners will be at last their strict ruler. We cannot believe in such a reversal of the activity of Him whom we know by the story of Christ.

It is little of Him that we know, but we are sure that the little we know will not be simply reversed afterwards. It will be developed in knowledge, it will not be contradicted, or at some dreadful moment declared out of date, when " He shall have put all things under His feet " and the robe of Mercy falls from Him as if it were a discarded disguise.

Our only hopeful line of inquiry is by way of parallel with the state and fortunes of the individual soul. What is it that Christ saves us for ? In conversion the soul finds the mercy of the Redeemer, but in that mercy he discovers discipline. Being reconciled, he does not fall upon a soft couch of self-pleasing, but is "quickened." Brought to newness of life, he becomes new in the spirit and alive unto God. He comes into no flowery path of moral indifference, but is raised to new heights of endeavour ; and the desire which animates and almost constitutes a new life inspired by our Lord is the desire of the kingdom and righteousness of God, that is to say, not a new and easy entrance into the privileges of the kingdom, or a mere imputation of the righteousness of God, but the establishment of His kingdom and the vindication of His righteousness, a vindication which requires in itself a real vengeance on our part upon our sins. Christ releases us, but He does not release us to a wilderness of self-will where we may roam according to our own changing desires, but to a home and a house of discipline, the home of the Father where is industry and honour. Or if, changing the image, we speak of our new status as enlargement, we enlarge from the present house of sin like a man who gets access to a mountain to pursue through toil and danger the white hart of virtue. Our forgiveness is a promotion and a restoration to more than the industry of the elder brother, to more than the heroism of another war. Christ thereby seals His choice of us to be His soldiers, and the road marked by His footsteps "winds upward all the way."

Now, what is true of the soul in this experience of pardon is true of a society which is conformed, or becoming conformed, to Christ. There will be in it two elements which at present do not wholly agree with one another. There will be an element of grateful humility, and there will also be an element of unsatisfied desire, the desire of virtue and honour, after the fashion of Him who died rather than that sin should in any wise prevail. Such a society, with great inconsistencies and many lapses, strives always to "rise on stepping-stones to higher things," to a more real peace, to a more secure partnership, to greater integrity, to the daily justification of a wider trust between man and man. It is the society itself, which, like the soul, enters upon the path of discipline, and the path of discipline is here and there the restriction or the exposure of the individual.

What is true of our particular social life is true of civilisation as a whole. Nor does history contradict this estimate of the meaning of national and international life. There is a progress; and while men seek for a test of progress in wider knowledge or in greater comfort they might well turn to measure this test, the test of greater and more justified trust, of fuller co-operation and more successful integrity.

We make progress slowly, whether in righteousness or in mercy; and while the progress is so slow and the position so low we cannot hope to see the synthesis of the two lines. It is only when righteousness and mercy reach their heights that they will be found to be one. Meanwhile, each effort, not only after mercy but after righteousness also, leads us to greater and more costly opportunities. Future difficulty and pain is the price we pay for past victory in either respect.

For, brethren, victory is much more costly than defeat, it is much more costly than neutrality. It does not win us a peace without effort, it drives us to exacting work for the reconstruction of society.

In the personal life, the man who is victorious over an early temptation finds himself confronted by temptations more seductive or more terrible; thus he is led by God from the parade-ground of good resolutions and good principles to the wind-swept heights of actual endeavour.

Now, we may say of our country and the civilisation we share that both of these are most securely themselves precisely when they are most nearly true to the Divine calling. And though we have no positive examples of success—whether in virtue or in tenderness—

we have a scale of differences along both lines which might well teach us that just when each is least untrue to Christ then it is most itself.

III. Meanwhile, we will avoid the dualism of despair. Sometimes the Christian nation has attempted to find a kind of stability in the creation of two organs, one for mercy and one for justice; one set of men, the ministers of Christ, who are to proclaim forgiveness with some indifference to justice, and another set of men who are to enforce virtue with some forgetfulness of mercy. Such a dualism is itself a halt in the large effort of which we have spoken and always fails, each of the several sides failing in its own appointed task. For what ministry of mercy could be maintained by men who are not perpetually sensitive to the difference between good and evil? and what ministry of justice can there be which is not constantly animated by a principle much more far-reaching than the punishment—or even the restraint—of the wicked; which has not its gaze constantly set upon the righteousness of a nation?

Now, in our own time, and no doubt in former times, there has been a wonderful advance at any rate in the mercifulness of justice, if not in the righteousness of mercy. Those who have had the opportunity of seeing at close quarters the work of the administration of justice know that it is ruled more and more clearly by the positive desire of holiness. They know how much wisdom is expended not merely in detecting the crime but in raising the criminal. How often, when the law would permit the passing of a heavy sentence, its ministers contrive a solution which is more just because it is more hopeful; and at the same time more merciful because it is more just! The administration of justice is, perhaps, at least as powerful in the improvement of our whole system of law as is any legislation or system of teaching, and that administration is on the whole leading us steadily step by step nearer to a real harmony between the awful beauty of holiness and the creative loveliness of compassion in Jesus Christ, the friend of publicans and sinners.

"THE LAME WALK"

THE REV. JOHN ALEXANDER HUTTON, M.A., D.D., EDITOR OF "THE BRITISH WEEKLY"

Educated at Glasgow University, Dr. Hutton was ordained to the Presbyterian Ministry in Alyth, Perthshire. Thereafter he ministered successively to Bristo Church, Edinburgh; Jesmond, Newcastle-upon-Tyne; Belhaven, Glasgow, and Westminster Chapel, London. From this last pastorate he was invited to become Editor of "The British Weekly." He has lectured frequently at Northfield, Mass., U.S.A. He has published many volumes, including "If God be for Us," "The Proposal of Jesus," "Discerning the Times," "The Persistent Word of God," "The Victory over Victory," "Our Ambiguous Life," etc., etc.

"THE LAME WALK"

BY THE REV. JOHN A. HUTTON, M.A., D.D.

"*The lame walk.*"—Matt. xi. 5.

THESE words occur as part of the answer which our Lord sent back to John the Baptist. John was lying in prison. He was there by the decree of Herod, who, you remember, had acted on the whim of a woman whom, with Herod, John had rebuked for the life they were leading. There he was in the prison of Machærus on the shore of the Dead Sea, his prison walls washed by the waves of its desolate waters. It is about as poignant an illustration as one could give of the *apparent* triumph of wickedness in this world. We can well believe that the brave man's heart was near to giving way. We conclude that so it was, from the question which he commissioned some of his disciples to put to Jesus. That question had to be a very direct one, one of those questions which admit of only the answer "yes" or "no."

The Baptist had to learn that you cannot get an off-hand, ready answer, an answer in terms of "yes" or "no," to any of life's really great questions. The answer from God to the great inquiries is never an unmistakable "yes" or "no," for that would destroy the soul, would interfere with our moral education. A "yes" spoken once for all by God to life's ultimate questions would paralyse our souls with a too great confidence; and a "no" spoken once for all to life's ultimate questions would paralyse our souls with despair. God's answer is never an explicit "yes" or "no," but only the secret pressure of His Spirit upon ours. The answer which Jesus sent back to the Baptist was of the same kind as God still sends back to all our questioning. "Art thou He that should come, or look we for another?" "Am I wrong in believing? Am I wrong in my estimate of Christ? And in that case, am I wrong everywhere?" And Christ's answer to him was, "The lame walk."

It was part of Christ's wonderful manner that He would not give Himself a name. It was His plan to be Himself, to become for man all that He could become, and leave it, not to the world as the world, but to those who in every age have been drawn to Him by secret and indestructible affinities, to *say* out what they have found Him to be. Jesus Christ is *there*: we see what He has been; we know what He has it in Him to be for this world of ours; and it is left to us to answer our own questions, and to say whether He is not for us the wisdom and the power of God.

My subject, however, is not that. I wish to consider, not the situation in which Christ used these words, "The lame walk," but these very words themselves. Obviously Jesus, in using such words in the circumstances in which He did use them, is describing what in His view was and is the characteristic feature or result of His appearance and work in the world of mankind. What is that characteristic feature?—"the lame walk!" That is to say, Jesus Christ came into the world to work a miracle. He came into the world to do something for man for which there was no other way. He came in order to break up the tyranny of all natural and moral consequences. He came in order so to deal with us that we one by one should have a new beginning. He came in order, if there should be need, to make an abrupt entrance into our lives, in order to plant something or Someone at the very root of our being, who should make all the difference in the world. When we keep back the miracle which Christ is ready to work, we are not faithful to Him.

It is perfectly true that the Christian religion assumes what in theology is called the doctrine of the Fall of Man. It assumes that in some profound way the race of mankind has gone wrong. For practical purposes it declares also that every one of us has in some way gone wrong ; or at least that there is something in each one of us which needs to be put right. There is something in each of us which might well be altogether different, stronger, steadier, holier. That—in one aspect of it—is the implication of the Fall.

I wonder what many people mean who become angry over that great doctrine. They say that it is a disparagement of man. I do not think so. It is a disparagement of you and me and everybody in particular, but it is not a disparagement of *man*, the child of God. On the contrary, the doctrine of the Fall is the doctrine of the essential dignity and erectness of man. Only he could fall who had it in him to stand erect. We must hold to the doctrine of the Fall if we are to hold to the doctrine of the essential and—God willing—the final erectness of man. The doctrine of the Fall simply declares that we men and women are naturally not ourselves, that we are not by nature, and can never by merely natural processes become, what God had in His mind when He proposed us. Is that a disparagement of men ? Do I disparage you if I say that you are not the man it is in you to be ? Do I disparage you if I tell you that God meant something bigger and better for you than, it may be, you are dreaming of? Would you rather I said that you are all the man you could ever have been, and that throughout eternity you will be the same? The only alternative to the Christian doctrine of the Fall—the doctrine that man has come down, and is not now himself—is the doctrine of human perfection. The alternative to the doctrine that we are naturally all wrong is the doctrine that we are all right. Now, if you tell me that I am all right I am depressed and miserable; for in that case life is a poorer thing than I had thought. But if you tell me that I am wrong, I ought at least to start up, either to answer you, or to examine myself, and if I find reason, I shall pray God to put me right.

To take an illustration which at the same time will lead us to the very text. Suppose I am walking behind someone whom I know, and presently I overtake him. I say, "I am glad to see you, and glad to see how briskly you can go along." Whereupon he looks at me displeased, and says: "Surely you cannot mean it. As a matter of fact I am going lame just now!" Why is the man displeased? Why is he right to be displeased? It is because I said something which meant that I thought he could walk no faster than he was walking, that I thought he was all right when he was not all right; and his displeasure at me is just the fine protest of a man against being taken for something no better than he seems, against being judged by his mere appearance, as though he could be nothing more. We may often have wondered that good people like our fathers could rejoice in the doctrine of the Fall. We need not wonder; they saw in it the deeper and the thrilling doctrine that, according to God's way of considering us, we are better than we have become, that our behaviour all along in this world has been, as we say, beneath us, not according to our dignity.

Now, Christianity is built round about that same doctrine. It declares that until we have been treated, until we have received from Christ something which He came to give to us, we all go lame. It declares that we are not ourselves until we are more than ourselves; and that we do not even begin to be ourselves until something has happened between Christ and our secret personality.

Let us keep hold of this idea of lameness as signifying of course that condition of moral impotence, of weakness and stumbling, or of dullness and deadness to God which is our average and natural condition until Christ makes us different. I mean now by "lameness," that, within each one of us in particular, which is hindering us from living our full, happy life as a child of God, under God's sky, with God's secret resource. Upon this, I can say what I have to say under four propositions:

(1) There are those who are *born lame.* "Man is born free, and everywhere he is in chains." So wrote Rousseau. The truth rather is: Man is born in chains, but our faith is that the heavenly powers are on the march to set him free. "Workers of the world, arise. You have nothing to lose but your chains!" So shouts Karl Marx. St. Paul's language is quite different and it is ultimately more respectful to man. "*Arise, shine, for thy light is come, and the glory of the Lord is risen upon thee!*" There is a sense in which it is the truth that we are none of us free and untrammelled, ready to run in God's ways, until Christ makes us free. But I am speaking now of varieties of this general

condition; and I say there are those who are born lame.

We have become aware in our day as never before of how the generations are bound to one another, how the sins of the fathers may be visited upon the children. I say, *may* be visited; and even the severest science cannot say more. Heredity—certainly on the moral side—is not a doom, but only a possibility. In a world governed by God we dare not say of anything evil that it *must* be. Indeed we dare say, on the contrary, of every evil that exists, that it need not be, that there are resources in God for its overthrow. Though it is only of recent years that we have learned so much of the material processes of heredity, the thing itself has always formed part of the knowledge of the human race. The Bible knows the doctrine that because "the fathers have eaten sour grapes, the children's teeth are set on edge." But the Bible declares that what God is working for in this world is to overthrow that fatal sequence. God is working for a state of things, as Jeremiah says, when everyone shall suffer for his own sin, and not for the sin of his fathers. And we believe that there is in Christ this very power to rescue every man from the dead hand of his ancestry. The great thinkers of Greece were engaged all the time with this very question—how was the evil which one generation had let loose in the world to be contradicted, transformed, brought to a standstill, and finally cast out? And it was given to them to see very deeply into that great inquiry. They saw, as in the *Antigone* of Sophocles, that if one of the fated line, even Antigone herself, were to allow that darkness to have all its way with her; if one were, in utter meekness and without one moment's revolt, to submit to the dark wave of evil consequence; that in her stricken soul the evil thing would die. Or, to put it otherwise, if one were to arise in the fated line who, by her passion to suffer, by her purity, by the sacrifice of herself in all her stainless beauty, would implant in the race a new and holy motive, *that* would counteract the fatal drift and change it into a tide towards God.

I verily believe that this has been done in Christ. Our fathers did well to protest that Christ had done something for the whole world of men, apart from what He could do for each of us, one by one. They did well to protest against Arminianism, and to claim for Christ's passion a worldwide and eternal significance. And it is when we think of hereditary evil that we seem to get a glimpse of that worldwide significance. In dying as Christ died, there was impregnated into the world of mankind a new motive ; there was let loose amongst the world-forces a new and blessed force—something which is now *there*, fighting against the tyranny of mere natural consequences ; something which each hard-pressed soul of man can lay claim to as a power on his own behalf, and also as a reason for believing that He who is with him is more than all that is against him !

I say there are those who are born lame. And Christ would fain make these walk and leap and sing. There is something that can come closer to us than the threatening of our natural blood ; it is the holy grace of the spiritual blood of Christ.

(2) And there are those who are *lame as the result of an accident*. There are those who to-day are what they are, and not better than they are, because of a sin, or because of a life of sin. They have done something wrong, something against the light, and they know it—and go lame. It may be that there is someone before

me in that very case. Well, if Christ cannot heal us, no one else can heal us. It is too great a subject to go into now—the subject of the possibility of forgiveness. I am here simply to say in Christ's name that everyone who sincerely repents of his sin, who bemoans it, who puts it in spirit away from him, and puts himself humbly in Christ's hands to bear witness to Him in the world—that every such one is forgiven, is back in the love of God. The Bible, the world, is full of such people, God be praised, whom Christ has healed of this kind of lameness —the lameness that comes with actual transgression.

(3) Then, again, there are those who are lame *because they are weary, because they are foot-sore.* They are getting older. Some of the visions of youth have failed. Life has broken for them some of its promises. The way for them now lies on a dead level of grey monotony, with no fine heights from which they can look beyond immediate things. It is the spiritual danger which besets us all from the mid-time of our life and onwards. And in the case of many there have been sorrows, disappointments from children, or disappointments from themselves, which have the effect of bringing them to a standstill. It is a bad form of lameness this. And yet with this also Christ can deal, making the lame ones walk. For the peril of our condition at such a time is that we consent to the view that because in some ways this life has failed us, all has failed. There is the danger, too, at this stage, that we lose something of our first natural heroism and that we fall into a mood desiring mere physical comfort, and estimating life by what it gives rather than by what it suggests and keeps in reserve. And Christ heals us of this lameness, in part, by arousing our minds to what is really happening within

ourselves. He came to show us that this world is not to be seen by itself, but always in its relation to another world and to God's will; that the things which are seen are temporal, and the things which are not seen are eternal. To the world's maxim that "nothing succeeds like success," He declares, on the contrary, that nothing fails like success. In His treatment of such cases, perhaps it is not His way now to thrill them into new life with some great and happy spiritual excitement, though He *may* choose that way; but rather to speak comfortably to them, to deal gently with them, to talk to them of other things, until, almost unknown to themselves, the lame begin to walk.

(4) I have spoken of those who are born lame, of those who have been made lame by accident, and of those who are lame because they are honestly tired and broken in spirit. There is yet another class of lame people in this world. They have become impaled upon a proverb: there are none so lame as those who will not walk. That is to say, there are those who are lame *because they are lazy*.

How does Christ deal with these? These must present to Him the hardest case. For their malady is in the region of *will*; and even God cannot, certainly He will not, compel the will. And yet surely there is in Christ something that should make these also get upon their feet and walk. The only hope for a lazy man is that one day he may become ashamed of himself. I verily think there was that, too, in Christ's purpose when He set His face to go to Calvary. I verily believe that He had it in His holy mind, by dying for man, to make us ashamed. Certainly that did happen. I think it is a fair thing to say that the first emotion which swept through the souls of the first disciples the moment they understood things, was a burning shame—shame that they had been talking about their own little affairs, as to who should get the best seat at table, and the best office in the new government; and all the while there was One beside them who saw no course before Him except to give up everything, even life itself. And surely there is still that in Christ which should shame us into protests against ourselves, when we consider that however we may sink back upon ourselves and humour ourselves in this world, there was One who heard in life a very different call.

Suppose we are standing on the bank of a river, when suddenly a child falls in and sinks. And we stand there doing nothing. But one of us steps out and plunges into the water to save the child. Suppose he saves the child. Do we not applaud his deed? Does not the most sluggish and worldly heart rise up to acknowledge an act like that which clothes our human nature with glory? And our applause, if it is genuine, is not mere applause. It is not mere admiration. It is the confession by every one of us who saw him do the deed that it was *our* deed; that in the deed he was our representative and substitute—not to spare us doing the like if the need should ever arise, but to create within hearts from which such an instinct is absent, and to augment in hearts where it already dwells, the instinct, in the presence of an occasion in which the very reality of the world of the spirit is at stake, to fling away our dearest thing, even life itself.

> The Son of God goes forth to war,
> A kingly crown to gain;
> His blood-red banner streams afar;
> Who follows in His train?

"COME UNTO ME"

THE REV. HUGH RICHARD LAWRIE SHEPPARD, C.H., D.D.

Late Vicar of St. Martin-in-the-Fields. Mr. Sheppard is the second son of the late Rev. Canon Edgar Sheppard. Educated at Marlborough, Trinity Hall, Cambridge, and Cuddesdon Theological College, Oxford. B.A., M.A., D.D. (Glasgow) 1927. *He became Secretary to the Bishop of Stepney,* 1905; *Chaplain, Oxford House,* 1907; *Deputy Priest-in-Ordinary to King Edward VII and to King George V; Head of Oxford House,* 1909–10; *Chaplain of the Order of St. John of Jerusalem,* 1910; *Extra Private Chaplain to the Archbishop of York,* 1911; *Priest in Charge of St. Mary's, Bourdon Street, and Grosvenor Chapel, South Audley Street,* 1911–14; *Chaplain of the Cavendish Club; Temporary Chaplain in France,* 1914; *Hon. Secretary of the Life and Liberty Movement; Select Preacher at Cambridge,* 1921; *Lecturer in Pastoral Theology at Cambridge,* 1921; *Proctor of the Diocese of London,* 1924; *Hon. Chaplain to H.M. the King,* 1916. *Among his publications are: "Two Days Before"* (*S.C.M.*) 1924, *"The Human Parson,"* 1924, *"The Impatience of a Parson." He is also Joint Editor of "St. Martin's Review."*

"COME UNTO ME"

BY THE REV. H. R. L. SHEPPARD, C.H., D.D.

"Come unto Me, all ye that are weary and are heavy laden, and I will give you rest."—Matt. xi. 28.

BEFORE I died, and if I had only one sermon more that I could preach, I should love to take this text as my subject. I have often tried to do so, but whenever I have made the attempt I have come down from the pulpit sad and ashamed and disappointed, knowing that I have never given to those wonderful appealing words the sense that our Lord would have given them. It is so difficult to preach from that text, and to be strong without being sentimental or emotional, and without merely offering a place of refuge to men and women who have not made good.

Yet in spite of this difficulty, I feel these words bring a message to life that at some time or another everybody needs, for even those who in a way have made the greatest successes in life at times realise that the success they have gained does not give them all that they ideally want. Take a successful business man after a day's success in the City: he has brought off a great stroke of business, his courage has justified his venture, his position has been established, and his name is on everyone's lips; yet he is weary with it all, unrested and unrestful, his life is a constant turmoil, he is pulled in all directions. How, he asks himself, can he go on being a success and realise his ideals? As he sits at the end of the day in his armchair over the fire, he may feel that he is standing at last on the pedestal of success, and yet that somehow he has missed the mark. Or take a successful society woman: she has hosts of friends, her entertainments and her clothes are chronicled in the woman's pages of the press, she has everything that wealth and position can give her; and yet there come to her moments in which it is no longer possible to keep thought at bay, when she wonders if all she has really satisfies her, and how long her present satisfaction is going to last when a sense of futility of life comes over her. "You have to keep going or you get left behind," said one such to me the other day. Or take, again, a boy and girl who have found that they are all in all to each other; as they look forward to the future, life seems to hold for them in their love everything they need, and yet even then there may be moments of misgiving, not that each should ever fail the other, but that all that each can give may not be all that they should for ever want. They may banish the subtle fear, but it will thrust up its head again and again.

It is to such as these, and to men and women of every class and type, that the message of my text comes; it can be universally applied and can be heard as a response to every aching longing from Park Lane to Whitechapel. It is just in these words that Christianity makes its most compelling appeal, an appeal utterly human, speaking to man as he really is, and offering him what he really wants as refuge and as salvation. For this reason the Christian preacher, if he had but one sermon more that he could preach, might surely desire to base that only sermon on this message of our Lord, wanting to emphasise the divinely human offer which his religion makes. He would want to say to all who heard him, and would want to say it to as many as he could reach: "Whatever your condition or your need, here is One who calls to you—your Saviour, your Lord, your King, your Companion, your Brother. To whosoever cometh, in whatever state he comes, from whatever distance he comes, He says, 'I will not cast you out.'"

So if I ask what is it that Christianity has and offers to every man that every other religion lacks, the answer to the question is quite simply, Jesus Christ. He is different from every other person in the world, and the deepest and the highest belief of Christianity is that Christ is the satisfaction of all men's needs, however different each may be mentally from the other, however incomprehensible they may be to their clergymen or their clergymen to them. The Christian preacher's message begins here, and in the end comes back to its starting-point, as he declares that once a human being takes that strong New Testament Figure as the director of his everyday life, he will not only get joy in living, not only power for his life, but will come into deeper truth about God. The preacher's message, I would venture to say, is borne out by the almost universal experience of men that to deepen the Christ-consciousness is to deepen the God-consciousness. For this reason, in what can any ordinary minister of the Gospel, conscious of the imperfection of his love, conscious of his infirmities and his lack of the knowledge of the full truth, glory more than in the power and the opportunity which are his to stand up before all men and offer them what as a matter of fact will and does satisfy their deepest yearnings, saying to all who will not only feel but think: "This is the message of my Gospel, this is the appeal of Christ: 'Come unto Me, all ye that are weary and are heavy laden, and I will give you rest' "?

But what do I mean as I repeat Christ's own invitation? What did He mean to those who were the first to hear the words from his lips? He did not mean, I am quite sure, that there was any special virtue in an act of physical approach to Him. That approach might only mean, and with many it was nothing more than, a movement of curiosity. To many in the crowd He was the latest sensation of the season. Christ never set Himself to satisfy idle curiosity, and He discouraged all sensation seekers. Such people as these might follow Him for a time, but that time was only short and they left Him as easily as they came. When He spoke, however, of people coming to Him, He meant, I think, some distinct effort of the will, however small the effort might be; He meant a readiness to take a definite step without knowing how far that first step might lead those who were prepared to take it; He meant an attitude of receptiveness from which prejudice and preconceived ideas were absent. I am led to think that this was His meaning, because He immediately went on to add to His invitation words which sound like a counsel rather than a command: "Take My yoke, and learn of Me," advice which might be taken or left, but which if followed would certainly result in that harmonious and balanced and satisfied life which He described as rest. The "coming" was only to be the first stage in the process of learning in which the willingness to accept and follow His teaching is described as the taking of the yoke; that is, in picturesque phrase, no longer to be one's own master, but to place oneself under another whose ideas should replace one's own.

When you come to think of it, that is a most tremendous demand, a demand that displays the supreme confidence of the speaker in Himself and that calls for equal confidence on the part of the learner in his teacher. But when you come to think of it again, it is only exactly the same demand that appears in every department of life's education. When you and I went to school or college, the only possible way in which our education could be attained, in which our own outlook on things in general or on any one subject in particular could be changed, in which our own imperfect and wrong ideas could be put right, was by placing our minds, so to speak, at the disposal of someone else, someone who was wiser and had a wider experience than ourselves. We could learn nothing whatever so long as we kept our minds shut against the penetration of any new ideas ; we could only gain the satisfaction and the sense of the mastery of all that life might contain for us in so far as we were ready to accept those ideas that at first certainly were not our own ; our education was not so much a matter of individual discovery as of experimentally practising what another told us, and which, when we put it into practice, we found to be true.

Now that, I believe, is exactly the same process that Christ so long ago had in mind when He said, "Come unto Me." The best fact about that message is that it is of universal application to every man and woman and holds good for all time. Nothing all down nineteen centuries has been added to what Christ said during three years in Judæa and Galilee ; all that saints and scholars and preachers have done has been to ring the changes upon the old and simple teaching of our Lord to His first disciples. They have drawn attention to what from time to time may have been overlooked, but to the essence of Christianity they have made no new contribution, nor have they ever suggested that anything was lacking in what Christ taught by the example of His life quite as much as by His words. Nor has anyone ever dared to suggest that anything might be lacking. Take any Christian creed you like, any book of religious devotions, any catechisms or formularies, articles or confessions of belief, however much the expressions and phrases of each may differ from another, they can each be directly related to the teaching of Christ, and none contain anything of Christian truth that cannot be found in the Gospels of the New Testament. That is why I think we need to get away from all that men, however wise, however saintly, have said about Christ, to the figure of Christ Himself as He stands out before the eyes of the world in all His wonderful simplicity at Bethlehem and Nazareth, in the wilderness and on the mountains, on Olivet and Calvary, at the open tomb and in the upper room. I believe that if a man would for the space of three weeks only honestly endeavour himself to live according to the Spirit of that life, if he would study that life, which, whatever may be the differences of interpretation, is perfectly plain and straightforward to him who would read it over without commentaries, and if he would set store not so much by the letter as by the spirit ; that man, I believe, would be lifted up to a high plane of living and achievement. His endeavour will involve him in immense hardship, but it will give him a satisfaction, a sense of rest that he will find nowhere else ; more than this, he will cause those who live with him and touch his life to realise that he has come to know the secret of noble living. Of this at least I am sure, that however far that man may come short of achieving his ideals, such a change will have taken place in his short life that never for one moment afterwards will he want to turn away from the path that he has begun to follow.

But I do not want you to be mistaken as to what it is that Christ offers those who come to Him. It is not, on the one hand, any relaxation from effort or any lethargic repose, it is not a life in which there shall be no difficulty or temptation or hardship. On the other hand, He is not referring to any place of rest beyond this life, beyond the grave, " where the wicked cease from troubling, where the weary are at rest," to any realms of bliss, those " pastures of the blessed " which the imagination pictures. What He offers has reference to the life which we are living on this earth to-day, to a life which for every one of us will probably have its full measure of outward distress and sorrow, of disturbance and misfortune. Life will have all these things, but Christ assures us—and the experience of hundreds of thousands now alive, and of hundreds of millions who are gone from our sight, tells us—that the assurance is not an empty boast, that with all that life may bring we shall find an inward peace of mind, a " rest to our souls." There will be no unceasing hurrying from one sensation to another, because we find that there is no stronger stimulus in life than that which we can find in Christ. There will be no vexation of spirit or jealousy of heart as we look from ourselves and our own circumstances to other people and their concerns, because in Christ we have come to see life in its true proportions, and to compare our lives with His and with none other. There will be no harassing anxiety for the future, either our own or that of those whom we love, because we know that Christ is our Companion all along the road. There will be no bothered worrying about theological questionings and disputes which we cannot understand, because we know that Christ stands behind all theology, and that He is simpler than the theologians would sometimes have us believe.

It is just this. But all that I have said or can say is entirely inadequate to express what Christ is to thousands who come and learn from Him. All I know is that I have not told and cannot tell one-thousandth part of what He is; but I know this too, that there is no emergency in life which with Him we cannot boldly meet; there is no problem to which He cannot supply the answer; there is no path so difficult, so intricate, so lonely, out of which He will not smooth the roughness and over whose pitfalls He will not safely lead us. If this is not rest, then I do not know what rest is; and if it is, then there is nothing else that I would so desire for myself, there is nothing which I would more desire to proclaim with my last breath to my fellow-men. "Come unto Me, all ye that are weary and are heavy laden, and I will give you rest. Take My yoke upon you, and learn of Me: and ye shall find rest unto your souls."

BREAD, WORK, AND LOVE

THE REV. G. A. STUDDERT KENNEDY, M.C.

Of Irish extraction, Geoffrey A. Studdert Kennedy was brought up in Leeds, where his father was vicar of a parish in a poor district. Kennedy was educated at Leeds Grammar School and Trinity College, Dublin. In 1908 *he was ordained by the Bishop of Worcester and went to work at Rugby under the present Dean of Windsor. He was eventually returned to assist his father in his slum parish in Leeds, and in* 1914 *he was appointed Vicar of St. Paul's, Worcester, a very poor parish of some* 3,000 *souls. He served as a temporary Chaplain to the forces on the Western Front from* 1916 *to* 1919 *and was awarded the Military Cross in* 1917. *He is at present Rector of St. Edmund the King and Martyr, Lombard Street, Chaplain to H.M. the King, and Honorary Messenger of the Industrial Christian Fellowship. Among his publications are: "The Hardest Part," "Lies," "Food for the Fed-up," "The Sorrows of God," "The Wicket Gate," "The Word and the Work."*

BREAD, WORK, AND LOVE

BY THE REV. G. A. STUDDERT KENNEDY, M.A.

"*Give us this day our daily bread.*"—Matt. vi. 11.
"*But My Father giveth you the true Bread.*"—John vi. 32.

ARE you afraid of poverty? I am. I have been all my life. I think that if we are honest with ourselves, most of us would confess to a fear of poverty. It is, next perhaps to the fear of death, the most prevalent and powerful of all the fears that haunt and hurt the lives of men and women in the world. Fear has always played a leading part in human life, and the fear of poverty is an ancient enemy. All down the ages men have struggled against it, and human history may well be viewed as the story of that struggle, a tragic and terrible story. That, stated in its simplest and most elementary terms, is what is now called the Materialist Conception of History. Those who take this view of life teach us that if we want to understand ourselves, and the changing history of man, his habits, customs, laws, institutions, his constant wars and his short, uncertain periods of peace, we must go right down to their roots, and there we shall always find one dominant and determining influence at work—daily bread, and the fear of being in want of it, the fear of poverty. It is, they say, the economic factor that is always final. Life, when you strip off the trimmings, is nothing but the struggle for bread.

Now, that seems to be a mean and sordid view of life, and we are tempted to turn from it, and dismiss it with disgust. And yet, if we are honest and courageous in our thought, we cannot help acknowledging that there is much truth in it, and without honesty and courage there is no hope of salvation either for our bodies or our souls. To quote a saying of Professor Huxley's: "There is no alleviation to the sufferings of mankind except through veracity of thought and of action, and the resolute facing of the world as it is when the garment of make-believe with which pious hands have hidden its uglier features has been stripped off." The struggle for bread is a fact, and we must face it and face it naked, stripped of the garments of make-believe that we too often weave in our own minds to hide it.

When we think of ourselves, you and I, and of our daily lives, there is nothing which in reality influences our thoughts and actions so much as the way in which we earn our living, struggle for our daily bread. For many, perhaps for most of us here, the struggle is in part disguised. We are not conscious of struggling with or against anybody else. We apply for, or are chosen for, a job, and we do it. We may do it for the most part without thinking of what we are to get out of it. It is our duty, and we may find much joy in it. We are paid for our work, but we do not work only, or even mainly, for our pay. We do not consciously struggle for bread. And yet there are facts behind our consciousness. If we lost the job, if the pay were delayed or cut in half, we should become vividly conscious of it. We should be, as we say, brought up against realities. We should become conscious of daily bread.

You applied for and got that job, and you were very pleased. You felt at peace with all the world. You got it. Somebody else did not. But he got something else. Perhaps he did. Perhaps he did not. He may be searching still. You were not conscious of cutting the other out. You did not want to cut him out. But you did. There was a struggle for bread. Sometimes even in these days you can see the struggle naked and without disguise, if you go and stand outside the dock gates at Liverpool and see the foreman come out to get men for a ship's unloading. There is a crowd of men always. More men than jobs. God only knows upon what principle or system they are selected. But watch the faces of those who are not successful, and you see the struggle for bread, naked, and in its nakedness pitiful. Naked or decently disguised, the struggle goes on. It always has gone on. All over the world. Throughout all time. Man with man, tribe with tribe, class with class, nation with nation, there always has been, there is now the struggle for bread, and behind it driving, goading, wounding, the fear of poverty.

In Africa to-day as the white man advances the native watches his lands grow less. The choice bits go to the stranger, the rough land goes to him. He sees the white tide rising, and watches it sullen and sad. There is the struggle for bread. It may be that the picture presented to us in Lord Olivier's *Anatomy of African Misery*, for instance, is overdrawn and inaccurate in detail, but I fear that there is no denying that in the main it is true. And, melancholy and distressing as it is, it is a mild and gentle story compared with the brutal and barbarous tales that could be told of the past.

How are we to reconcile this age-long and world-wide struggle for bread with the picture of our Father's love which is the essence of the Gospel of Jesus Christ? Is the world a home or a battlefield? Is life a struggle or a gift? Is the Gospel picture itself just a golden garment of make-believe with which pious hands have sought to hide the ugliness of the struggle for bread? Must we, if we be honest, tear that garment away and be content to look upon the naked fact? That is a question which, in a thousand different forms, presents itself to Christians of to-day. Can we face the facts of life and still believe in our Father? God does not give us bread. We have to struggle for it. We must either earn it or steal it; there is no third alternative. If a man will not work, neither shall he eat. That is the law of life. Those who strive to evade that law are thieves. There are the sick, the aged and infirm, and the children, and to them we feel it is right that we should give their daily bread.

But there is something degraded and degrading about giving bread to those who ought to earn it. There is something wrong about begging. Giving away money, or bread for which money stands, is one of the most difficult and dangerous things in the world to do. Even when a brother begs for what he ought to earn, a man might very well hesitate for fear of doing harm. There are men and women we would like to help, and we know they need it, but we dare not offer to give. They are what we call proud. They have a strong conviction that they ought to earn. God does not give us bread. There never was a harvest on the earth until men learned to work together. Men may hunt and kill alone, but they must sow and reap together. It was work that taught us love. That is the other side of the picture. Men have learned to love each other by working together for bread. There is, and there has been, a struggle for bread, but the struggle never made the bread; it has always meant work, and work is the author of love. Husband and wife were first of all workmates. They came together to work for their children, and by working learned to love. The family was a working unit, and is a working unit still.

For thousands of years it was the chief working unit. All labour centred round the home, and the only love there was on earth was found within the home. Men loved their own kith and kin, but outside that narrow circle the world was full of enemies. But slowly the working unit widened as men learned to trade with and work with their neighbours. Then neighbour-love began. It grew very slowly. Men were suspicious of one another and afraid. They distrusted strangers and did not willingly combine. Often they fought one another bitterly before they settled down to work together. But always as they worked together love and friendship grew. And as the working unit widened, wealth increased and the harvest was more plentiful. For the more men work together, the richer the harvest grows. Love is the real source of wealth. It has not been a smooth and easy process this ; it has been checked and broken a million times. It is checked and broken still. The old hatreds and suspicions, the old fear of strangers and dislike of foreigners, persist and constantly tend to break the wider working unit up or prevent us making it. But in spite of apparently insurmountable obstacles the majestic process persists. The working unit widens, and with it grows the sweep of neighbour-love. God's plan and purpose for the world are being wrought out through work. He has taken a great step forward in these latter days. The working unit has, with almost dramatic suddenness, widened out until, for the first time in history, it includes the entire world. The harvest for which you meet to render thanks at this Festival of Harvest is the harvest of the world.

But a few years back a summer such as we have had would have set the ghost of famine walking through our villages and towns. But our harvest-fields are wider now, and we reap from all the world. God has spoken and decreed that from henceforth all men and women, east, west, north, and south, over the length and breadth of the earth, should be workmates, and by working together learn to love. It is in some ways a terrible decree, because we are not ready for it. Our old habits and inherited ways of thought die hard. We still want to be independent and work away at our own little plot. We will try to conquer one another, and pretend that we do not need one another. We break out into squabbles and fights, and the feet of warring armies trample down the golden corn and lay waste the smiling summer lands. We still are savages at heart, suspicious, mistrustful, stubborn, and very much afraid. We wave our flags and beat our drums, and threaten one another at home and abroad. We organise ourselves into independent cliques, classes, and nations, and stand up for our rights. On the surface it would seem as though God's decree were causing more hatred than love. But all this fretting and fuming is vain. God has spoken, and we shall be one. Slowly and painfully, but surely too, we are learning our lesson, the lesson of universal love. We may, like petulant children, beat with our puny fists against the majestic arms of God, but they close, and keep on closing without haste and without hesitancy.

Those who hold to the materialist conception of history and see at the root of all man's life the struggle for bread are, I believe, right in their facts, but wrong in the meaning they give to the facts. They do not overrate the importance of the economic factor in human evolution, but they do misinterpret it. They do not understand the meaning of bread. They think of bread in terms of struggle, whereas it should be thought of in terms of work, and then of love. They think bread means war, when in truth it means peace. This they do because they fall into the special pitfalls which the theory of evolution always contains for careless thinkers. The study of human evolution leads men to concentrate their minds upon the origins of man. They turn back to the past and saturate their thought with pictures of primitive life, primitive habits, customs, and laws. The past tends to become an obsession with them, and they try to " explain " the present in the " light " of their obsession. But " if the light that is in thee be darkness, how great is that darkness."

Used in this way, the historical method becomes a blight and a curse to human thought. It keeps us with our mind's eyes fixed constantly upon the past. It forces us to go upon our way looking where we are coming from. That is fatal. It leads to paralysis of the will. We cannot live, any more than we can walk, looking backwards all the time. We must not keep our mind's eye in the back of our heads. It is not the past which explains the present, it is the present which explains the past. You cannot explain a man by studying a baby; you can only explain a baby by studying a man. This might seem, too, an obvious error, but it is so common as to be almost universal, and it is impossible to overestimate the evil that it does. A great part of the conflict between Religion and Science is due to the instinctive rebellion of Religion against the misuse of the historical method, which keeps the present and the future bound helpless to the past, and seeks to "explain" and evaluate the higher in terms of the lower, mind in terms of matter, life in terms of mechanism, freedom in terms of necessity, the human in terms of the animal. It is not against Darwinian facts that Religion protests, but against Darwinian values, or, it would be more accurate to say, pseudo-Darwinian values. Darwin himself was too great a scientist to pretend that he dealt with values at all.

The materialist conception of history, which seeks to explain life in terms of hunger and the struggle for bread, is a particular and pernicious instance of this fallacy. Men are taught to explain the present in terms of the past. Look back, and you see a struggle between tribes, nations, and classes, a constant struggle for bread. The economic factor always has been final and decisive, therefore the struggle must continue and the economic facts always will be final and decisive. The minds of men are concentrated upon and hypnotised by the past, and the blackest features of the past, and thus their faith in the future is paralysed and perverted. Against this ruinous disease of the mind and spirit, Christian thought protests. It seeks to explain bread in terms of man, and not man in terms of bread. It thinks of human evolution always as an ascension.

That figure of the Perfect Man with wounded hands outstretched to bless ascending to His glory dominates and controls our view of evolution. The hands are wounded, for the struggle was a reality; but they will not always bleed, because love triumphs in the end. He is the true meaning of bread. Bread means work, and work means love, the true love which began and begins at home, but ends by filling all the world and making all mankind a family. It is with our eyes fixed upon the future that we pray, " Give us this day our daily bread "—not merely that we may be fed, but that the Father's name may be hallowed, His Kingdom come, His will be done on earth as it is in heaven. It is with our eyes fixed upon the future that we stretch out our hands and take into them a piece of Bread, which, because in loving fellowship we have offered it up as all bread should be offered up, means Christ, and helps to make that meaning part of the very substance of our souls. For the Kingdom of God comes not by sword or strife, nor yet by sitting still, but as men learn to will and work together in ever-widening fellowship and in the spirit of Him who came not to be ministered unto, but to minister—who is the true meaning of Bread.

THE RIGHT TO BE HAPPY

THE REV. LAWRENCE PEARSALL JACKS, D.D., LL.D., D.Litt.

Dr. Jacks was educated at University School, Nottingham; the University of London; Manchester College; Göttingen and Harvard (U.S.A.). He entered the Ministry as Assistant to the Rev. Stopford Brooke at Bedford Chapel in 1887, and subsequently became Minister of Renshaw Street Chapel, Liverpool, and the Church of the Messiah, Birmingham. Since 1903 he has been Professor of Philosophy, and since 1915 Principal of Manchester College, Oxford. He has edited the "Hibbert Journal" from its foundation in 1902. Amongst his publications are: "Life and Letters of Stopford Brooke," "Mad Shepherds, and other Human Studies," "Among the Idolmakers," "All Men are Ghosts," "Religious Perplexities," "The Life of Charles Hargrove," "Constructive Citizenship."

THE RIGHT TO BE HAPPY

A Sermon to Boys on a Wet Day

BY THE REV. L. P. JACKS, M.A., LL.D., D.Litt.

PREFACE

"IT is easy to preach a good sermon; but difficult to preach a sermon that does any good." This remark was once made to me by an eminent preacher with a well-established reputation for "good sermons," good in many senses of the term. He had preached so many of them, and been at it so long, that we may presume he knew very well what he was talking about. I think the remark profoundly true. For there is a great difference (as Christ Himself seems to have discovered) between *teaching* a thing and *getting that thing learnt*; between piping and getting people to dance to the tune; and a still greater difference between teaching a truth and *getting it acted upon*. "Why call ye Me, Lord, Lord, and do not the things that I say?" For more than nineteen centuries Christendom has been calling Him "Lord, Lord," but not doing the things that He said.

I will venture to expand the saying just quoted from the distinguished preacher: "It is easy to preach a good sermon, but difficult to preach a sermon that *does no harm*." Now, a sermon may do harm in many ways. It may do harm, of course, by teaching false doctrine; though it is comforting to reflect that much of the false doctrine we teach, like much of the true, is not *learnt*—for Satan (thank God) has his half-hearted disciples as well as Christ. But a sermon can also do harm by preaching true doctrine in a way which sets people against it—I can remember sermons which have done me harm in just that way. A preacher who preaches true doctrine ought to have a taking and convincing way with him, which not many of us have; otherwise he may do more harm than good. He will do harm if he *bores* people; or if they cannot hear what he says and lose their tempers; harm if he leaves them with the impression that he himself doesn't quite believe what he is saying, but only wants them to believe it—and in many other ways that need not be named. Another distinguished preacher, an American, after preaching one of his finest sermons to an enormous congregation, came into the vestry where the deacons were waiting to congratulate him, and, flinging his manuscript on the table, exclaimed, "Well, thank God, I don't think *that* can do harm to anybody." Let us hope he was right.

In my time I have preached an enormous number of sermons on an enormous variety of subjects. Most of them have gone up the chimney; for I have come to a time of life when it behoves me to ask myself what will become of that vociferation when I am dead. And now the Editor challenges me to select, out of the remnant that remains, one that will bear confronting with the title: "If I had only one sermon to preach." Was preacher ever faced with a challenge so formidable?

The rule I have set myself in making the selection is this: to find a sermon, if I can, that I have reason to believe did *good* and no reason to believe did *harm*. That, if I can find it, is the sermon that I would like to go on preaching, if I had only one sermon to preach.

I have preached many sermons (may the All-compassionate look upon them in mercy!) much " finer," much more " beautiful," than this one. Most of them have gone up the chimney with a multitude less " beautiful " and less " fine." But I believe, on evidence that seems to me convincing, though I dare say others would not find it so, that this one has done some good; and I have no reason for thinking that it has done any harm. I have often preached it, mostly to audiences of young people; in boys' and in girls' schools, in men's and in women's colleges, in Great Britain and in America, sometimes as a sermon with a text (there are scores in the Bible to choose from), oftener as an " address "; and I intend to go on preaching it as long as I live. Sometimes I have wrapped it up in stories, which the critics say is bad art. And once or twice I have made it the subject of philosophic writings which other critics tell me are bad philosophy. Plainly it has done the critics good. It has never been printed in the newspapers, though a bit of it torn out of its context did get into the *Daily Mail* and brought me many letters of remonstrance, the tenor of which only proved, so I thought, that it had done the remonstrants good.

Strictly speaking, this sermon is not about religion at all. But then I happen to be one of those who think that the direct way of teaching religion is not the best way. The best way of teaching religion (I think) is *indirect*. There is only one direct teacher of religion—that is God, or, as I prefer to call Him, the Holy Spirit. We human teachers succeed best, by which I mean getting the thing *learnt* and not merely *taught,* when we practise indirection; which, by the way, seems to have been the method of Christ, who never once mentions the word

" religion "—happily for religion the word was not much in use in His day. Certainly if I had only one sermon to preach it would not be one of those in which I have tried—for I *have* tried it—the direct method. To the chimney with all those, " fine " as some of them are, or were said to be by ladies in the congregation!

I might be hard put to it if the reader were to press for the reasons which have led me to believe that this sermon has done good. I cannot promise that it will do *him* any good; nor even that it will do him no harm; so perhaps he had better skip it and read the others in the volume. I can only assure him that it has done *me* good to preach it; because I know that it contains something that I really believe myself, and not merely something that I want other people to believe—though I do want them to believe it too. The other evidence I possess of the sermon having done good is much too private to be communicated to the reader. It consists of the confidences of certain young friends of mine, mostly in England and America (one in Patagonia), which nothing would induce me to betray. They may trust me to keep their secret.

THE RIGHT TO BE HAPPY

There is no doubt a feeling in your minds of a want of harmony between the subject on which I am announced to speak and the weather which Providence has seen fit to send us. A fine day would be more appropriate to a talk about happiness. But I am not so sure about that. There is a sort of happiness that consists in feeling that you can afford to do without it. And that is a feeling we old fellows often get. We learn to take our happiness much as we take the weather, thankful for it when it comes fine, but not making a fuss when it doesn't. My own opinion is that the right to happiness and the right to fine weather stand on about the same level. Strictly speaking, they are not rights at all. We have to take both things, both happiness and weather, as they come. Unless we can be cheerful in bad weather, our cheerfulness in good weather won't amount to very much. In the same way I am inclined to think that nobody can be very happy in life until he has learnt to bear a lot of the other thing without making a fuss about it. So you see the weather to-day is rather appropriate to my subject than otherwise.

It has often been remarked that anybody who talks about happiness is sure to get himself into difficulties. If you talk against it, as I rather think I am going to do, people will immediately jump to the conclusion that you want to make them miserable, and that will set them against you from the outset. If you talk in its favour and praise it up, people will tell you that your notion of happiness is different from theirs and that what would be Paradise to you would be a place of torment to them. Men in general are not good judges about their own happiness, and they are still worse judges about the happiness of other people. A large part of our miseries are the direct result of mistaken attempts to make ourselves happy. And it must be confessed that our attempts to make other people happy do sometimes turn out dismal failures. On the whole, I am inclined to think there would be far more happiness for all of us if we put it out of our minds and gave our thoughts to other and more important things.

The promotion of happiness is of course a very

beautiful occupation, if you look at it in the abstract. But in practice it gives rise to an enormous amount of fraud. The swindler always begins by pretending that he is going to make you happy, and if you are the kind of person who makes his own happiness the first consideration, you are just the man for the swindler to practise upon. And so in general an age like our own, which has made happiness into a kind of god, is an age which is certain to get itself frightfully swindled. The art of advertisement largely consists in persuading people that they have only to buy the advertiser's goods, his hairwash or his cigarettes or his whisky, or what not, and they will forthwith find themselves in the seventh heaven of happiness. The demagogue, who is a much more dangerous person than the advertiser, works the same string. He gains his following by dangling before the eyes of the public a vision of happiness that can never be fulfilled. Yes, the promotion of happiness is a beautiful thing in the abstract. But let us beware of the people who offer to promote it in the concrete. Most of them are trying to lead us by the nose, a thing which is easily done in an age which worships happiness as a god.

An immense amount of misery is caused in the world by people who think they have a right to be happy always, so that if they chance to be unhappy, they jump to the conclusion that somebody has been doing them a wrong, and begin hunting about for the villain who has done it, blaming society, blaming the Government, blaming the age in which they live, because they are not as happy as they think they have the right to be. Those are the most unpleasant kind of people in the world—the squealers, I call them. I have heard it said by foreigners that one of the finest qualities of the English character lies in the way it stands up to unhappiness. Mr. Walter Page, the famous American Ambassador, who was such a good friend to England during the war, paid us the high compliment of saying that the English were not a nation of squealers. He was constantly writing letters to President Wilson about the way the English people stood up to the unhappiness of that terrible time, especially about the splendid women, the mothers and wives and sisters, who had lost those who were dearest to them, whose hearts were broken, perhaps, and yet never uttered a complaint.

Nobody has the right to be happy always. Nobody can be. You can't be happy when people you are fond of *die*—and you have no right to be. You can't be happy when you see your friends in misfortune—and you have no right to be. Nobody was meant to be happy *always*. If you study the human body, the way it is built up, you will see at once that happiness is by no means the only thing it is made for. The human body is a wonderful instrument for doing things with, the difficult things too. The hands, the eyes, the brain, the bones, the muscles, all show that the human body has been built up not for pleasure but for action—for standing strains, for carrying burdens, for embarking on dangerous expeditions, for all kinds of skilful and delicate and heroic operations—quite as much for bearing pain as for enjoying pleasure.

There was an ancient philosopher who said that very clearly; you older boys will make his acquaintance when you go to the University if you have not done so already. His name was Aristotle. Aristotle had a good deal to say about happiness—though he didn't mean by the word what most people mean when they use it to-day. But he saw that man is cut out not so much for happiness as for action, for *work,* as we should say, for difficult, skilful, beautiful work. And the only way to get happiness is by doing the work you are fitted for in the best manner it admits of. That is what Aristotle said, and that is what I am going to repeat to you to-day.

Looking back on the happiness I have had in life—and I have had my fair share of it, and many kinds of it—I think I can say that the best of it has come from the work I have had to do, and from the people who have helped me in doing it. Unless a person is happy in his work you can't make him very happy in anything else, though perhaps he may think you can. Holidays and play are good—no one has enjoyed them more than I have—but holidays and play don't amount to much unless they have a background of enjoyable work behind them. Don't suppose for a moment that I'm out against play—nobody believes in it more than I do. But I can't agree with those people who make out that work and play are opposites one to the other. In all good work there's a certain element of play; and in all good play there's a certain element of work—as you find out whenever you play a football match against a team that's worth playing with. Those people make a big mistake who think that play is all happiness and work is all misery. There's a great difference between playing and fooling. There's a great difference between playing the game and playing the fool. I will tell you who the people are who know most both about work and about play. They are the *artists,* the people who create beautiful things, fine buildings, fine music, fine poetry, fine painting and sculpture.

The artists: I should like to say a word about them, because I think they are almost the most important people in the world—next to boys and schoolmasters! Sometimes you hear artists spoken of as though they were only the people who make ornaments, pretty things to hang on the wall or to put on the mantelpiece. Well, they wouldn't be very important if they only did that. If that was all they did we might manage to get on without them. But they do a great deal more than that. They do something that we cannot get on without. Art is only work excellently done, and the artists are the people who do their work better than the rest of us are doing ours. I don't care what you are doing—I don't care what your work is—it may be translating a piece of Cicero into good English, or it may be playing a football match, or making tables and chairs, or it may be running the finances of a bank—I say that you have only to do the job just as well as it can be done and you will make a work of art of it, and you will become an artist in that line.

You will become an example, too, and when other people see you doing your job in that excellent way, they will become a little envious of you, and they will go away wishing there was anything in life they could do half as well—and a mighty good thing it is for them to be made to feel like that. That is one reason why artists are such important people. They make other people wish they could do their own jobs as well as the artists do theirs. I confess that I feel that way whenever I listen to a great pianist or to a master of the violin, like Kreisler, whom I heard not long ago. "Ah!" I say to myself, "if only I could do my job as well as that, if only I could write books or preach sermons as well as that fellow plays a fiddle, what books they would be! All the world would rush to read them! What congregations I should have!" How delightful it must be to be able to do your job in that way—to translate Cicero as well as that, or play football as well as that, to make chairs and tables as well as that. And yet, what is the man doing? He's just *playing*—playing the fiddle—not playing the fool. If I were to say the man is *working* his fiddle, you would think it a very odd expression. But why shouldn't I say he is working his fiddle? It has taken him years of hard work to learn to play like that. But don't you see what has happened? The man's work has become so fine that it has turned into beautiful play. He worked his fiddle right enough when he was learning his notes, as anybody would have known who had listened to the horrible sounds he used to make in those days. But now the work is done so well that when we hear it we call it play—playing the fiddle. Where, then, is the difference between work and play? I tell you the difference is not as great as people think it is. The best work is always a kind of play; and the best play is always a kind of work. We call it art, and the people who do it we call artists. There's no mystery about art or about artists. Art is excellent work, and artists are excellent workers—that's all. You see now why I rate them among the most important people in the world.

And they are not only among the most important, but I believe they are the happiest as well. The happiness comes out of their work, and their work is so well done that it becomes a kind of play. I never knew an artist—and I have known a good many—who didn't thoroughly enjoy his work, who wasn't glad when the day's work began and sorry when it came to an end. What a good thing it would be if all the work of the world was like that. It might be. Perhaps some day —though not for a long time—it will be. My notion of the Kingdom of Heaven is just that: a state of things when everybody is glad when the day's work begins and sorry when it ends.

And that leads me to say another thing about happiness. As far as I can make it out, there are two main kinds of happiness: the first is the kind that is given to us by other people, and the second is the kind we create for ourselves. I've had both kinds in my life; and my experience is that the kind of happiness we make for ourselves is more real and more lasting, and on the whole more worth having, than the kind which other people make for us and give us for nothing— though that also is very good in its way. Of course we all know what a fine and noble thing it is to make other people happy—we ought to do it whenever we can. But for my part I don't want all my happiness to be made for me by other people. I don't want to be dependent on others for my happiness, however kind and good they may be. I don't want to get into the habit of calling upon other people to make me happy. I should like to be able to make the main part of my happiness for myself. In fact, I'm inclined to think that unless I make the greater part of my happiness for myself, what other people can do for me in that line won't amount to very much.

A person who is happy only when other people make him so is really a very miserable sort of person, and there are a lot of them about—people who expect to be made happy by the State, or by the Government, or by the social system, or by their friends and neighbours in general, and who go about complaining and whining because other people are not making them as happy as they think they have the right to be. I hope there are none of that kind in your school, though it's a highly exceptional school if there are not. Nobody enjoys an occasional treat given him by other people more than I do. But what kind of a person is it who can only be happy when somebody else is giving him a treat? What kind of person is it who wants his life to be a kind of picnic to which other people are always inviting him? I will tell you. That person is a moral baby. He is not a boy and not a man.

I believe that nobody can be really happy in this world unless he makes the greater part of his happiness for himself. And I will tell you another thing about that. The people who can make happiness for themselves are generally the very ones who help to make others happy at the same time. Think of the artist I was just speaking about. Think what a lot of happiness he makes for himself by his work; and then think what a lot he makes for other people at the same time by those beautiful things that he creates—by his music, or his singing, or his poetry, or his painting, or whatever else it may be. If you will take a word of advice from an old fellow like me, let me offer you this. If you want to be really happy, learn to make the greater part of your happiness for yourselves and not to be dependent on treats given you by other people.

But how can you do that? Well, there is one word that answers the question. The word is "skill"—a word which ought to have a greater place in education than it has. I know that word won't satisfy everybody.

They will want me to use another word—" kindness," for example; but kindness is only a rare sort of skill in dealing with other people. Or " goodness"; but goodness is only a rare kind of skill in doing right. I give the word " skill" without any apologies, and I give it a very wide meaning; there is skill of the heart, skill of the brain, skill of the voice, skill of the hand. And I say this, that without skill of one kind or another nobody can be really happy. By acquiring skill in one or other or all these ways we acquire the means of making our happiness for ourselves instead of being dependent for it on other people—as nobody ought to be. Skill in work that makes it a kind of beautiful play, skill in play that makes it a kind of beautiful work —that is the great source of happiness for everybody, old and young. I think that nobody's education is complete unless it leads him to acquiring some kind of skill—and there are a thousand kinds of it.

But what is skill? How shall we define it? Skill, I take it, is simply *wisdom in action*; knowledge completing itself by doing the thing that it knows. Until our knowledge has turned itself into skill of one kind or another, it is a half-grown thing; it will be forgotten, it will die without bearing any fruit. And the main fault I have to find with our educational system at the present day is that it imparts knowledge up to a point, and then stops short without turning it into skill, so that the pupil goes out into the world unequipped for any kind of socially valuable occupation, ready for nothing that would give him a sense of his personal usefulness to the world. The idea of vocational training has been overdone, or rather it has been narrowed down to the purely economic sense. But if you mean by it the kind of education which equips the pupil for a socially valuable occupation and so gives him the sense of his personal value to society, then I would say vocational training is right. Our object should be not so much to make education vocational, but to make vocations educational. It will be so in the Kingdom of Heaven. In the Kingdom of Heaven every man will put God (who is the Supreme Excellence) into his daily work, thereby converting his work into beautiful play and himself into the kind of person whom others can love.

To the young people who hear me to-day I would say this: When the time comes for choosing your vocation, choose one that challenges your skill; choose one that will put your mind, your whole personality, *on its mettle*: the happiness best worth having is to be found on those lines. Beware of soft jobs. Don't listen to the people who tell you that man was made for happiness. He wasn't. He was made for doing difficult, beautiful, heroic work, and the only happiness he is entitled to is the happiness that comes from doing it.

"MY GOSPEL"

THE REV. FREDERICK WILLIAM NORWOOD, D.D., CITY TEMPLE, LONDON

Born in Australia, he was educated at Ormond College, Melbourne, and is an Honorary Captain of the Australian Imperial Force. He was called to Churches at Canterbury (Victoria), Brunswick (Victoria), and North Adelaide (South Australia). Since 1919 *he has occupied the pulpit of the late Dr. Parker, at the City Temple, London. He is the author of "The Cross and the Garden," "Sunshine and Wattlegold," and "Moods of the Soul."*

"MY GOSPEL"

BY THE REV. F. W. NORWOOD, D.D.

"*According to my gospel*" (a frequent saying of St. Paul's).

THERE is all the difference in the world between a religion and a gospel.

Religions are as thick as autumn leaves. Almost every man is compelled to shape out one for himself, in which traditional and personal elements may be strangely mingled. But not every religion could be called a gospel. Indeed, broadly speaking, that title is reserved for the Christian faith.

Christianity did not appear in the world as a new *religion*, but as "glad tidings." It brought men a message of "peace and goodwill" from God. It offered hope of deliverance to all men from sins and sorrows which are shared alike by all. That was the secret of its power. If it has lost its grip upon us to-day—as indeed it has upon many people—it is because we have missed, or do not believe, its essential message.

Christianity had no radical quarrel with the ancient Judaism out of which it emerged.

Jesus Himself was born of the Jews, and was a true "Son of the Law." He claimed to be in line with all the prophets. He did not ask His disciples to break with the ancient faith. He was sure that certain things which were implicit in Judaism had come to their fulfilment in Himself. His one and only aim was to bring men into such relation with God as would give them deliverance from their sins, peace within their consciences, joy and power in heart and life.

This left Him still a Jew, but with a mesage and outlook which far transcended Judaism. He reached out to all men. He refused to be circumscribed by any traditional or ritualistic limitations. His province was the universal heart of man. " Neither in this place nor yet in another shall ye alone worship God. Ye shall worship the Father in spirit and in truth. The Father seeketh such to worship Him. God is Spirit; and His worshippers must worship Him in spirit and reality."

He never criticised a single form or ceremony. He aimed no polemical shafts at any form of religion whatsoever. He saw the universe as one. He saw the universal heart of man as one, in spite of all its superficial differences.

God loved man everywhere and always. Wherever he was to be found, man was hampered by his sins, confused by his thoughts of the Creator, and of life both here and hereafter. Christ came not to condemn, but to save. He brought good news of God, and revealed the life, the truth, and the way. He called His message the Gospel, which means " good news."

The first disciples were much narrower in their thought and outlook than He. Not all at once did they perceive the universal application of His message. They tried to compress it within the limits of the faith in which they had been bred. They did not believe at first that the Gentiles had an equal share in the " good news."

But the new wine was too strong for the old bottles. Their message fretted itself out of its confinement by the force that was in it. Once they believed in the love of God, they could not set boundaries to it. Because their field was the heart of man, stripped of all accidents of birth and breeding, they found it everywhere the same, full of sorrow, conscious of failure, longing for peace and assurance.

They tried to express their convictions as best they could. Naturally they fell back upon figures and illustrations. Just as naturally they found them in the faith in which they had been brought up. This was wise and necessary also, because the minds of their hearers could easily grasp them. That is why there are in the New Testament so many allusions to the sacrifices of the Temple and so many references to the Old Testament Scriptures. They were most helpful to the original hearers of the message, though they may be confusing to the modern mind.

Men have been doing the same thing ever since. There has been one experience running through the Church in all ages, but the methods of interpretation have been different.

The basic element in the human heart has always been the same. Man has always been full of sorrow and failure while longing for peace and assurance.

That is why we have had so many varying explanations of the Fall and the Atonement. Some of them seem grotesque and even horrible to-day, but in their own day they were powerful and convincing. Instead of their variety convincing us that they were false, we ought rather to think how deep and universal is the human need which has so many facets.

There will be many more yet. Life is always changing. Knowledge grows, experience widens, but the human heart changes little. We are still full of sorrow, conscious of failure, and longing for peace. We still need "good tidings of God." What we are needing is not a new evangel, but the appropriate interpretations and illustrations which, as one has said, "would be to us as absolute a solvent of our difficulties about life as Christianity was to the difficulties of the early Christians."

Ask yourself these questions: Are our human sorrows less to-day than they were? Has science or philosophy delivered us from the fact and feeling of failure? Do we need peace and assurance less or more than our fathers did?

Let us strip religion to its kernel. Would it not be well if we could believe that God has goodwill and even love toward His creatures? Do we not need some positive and even objective assurance that our sins and failures—so real a part of our lives, but so irrevocable in their nature—can be and are, to use a scriptural phrase, "removed from between us and God"? Do we not need peace and confidence concerning the future, both in this world and in that other world which persists in haunting our minds? And do we not need some spiritual enabling so that we may here and now live in harmony with our hopes and in assurance of final victory?

These things are the essential content of Christianity. They form its essential substance. They constitute it a gospel of good tidings.

The form under which we interpret and explain them varies constantly and will continue to vary. Even under imperfect forms, men have felt their power. In every changing century, believers have experienced their moral and spiritual enrichment. They are doing so still. Those who to-day are assured of the saving power of the faith would have to explain their assurance in terms which would have been foreign to Wesley or Luther or Savonarola or St. Francis of Assisi, or, perhaps, to St. Paul. But we cannot surrender them. If we do, we may have Religion, but we have not a Gospel.

Some of us devote our whole lives to the attempt to explain these things of which we are personally sure. Our own explanations have undergone many changes even within the compass of our short experience, but the basic reality has not altered.

Do not fasten your attention upon some explanation of the Atonement which satisfied your fathers but does not satisfy you. Before Copernicus, men explained the movements of the heavenly bodies differently from what they do now, but the stars persist in their courses as of old. You still need God. "We are no better than our fathers," as the prophet sobbed so long ago. Life sweeps us on towards that "bourne from which no traveller returns." We need peace and assurance. The right pronunciation of the word "Atonement" is At-one-ment. Our greatest need is to be at-one with God.

Hearken still to Jesus. There are many religions, but what we need is a gospel. Give renewed attention to Jesus. "The Lord hath yet more light and truth to break forth from His holy Word."

Let me try if I can put what seems to me to be the essential content of the Christian Gospel inside the compass of a single address. It is of course an impossible thing to attempt, but let it go for what it is worth.

I will state it baldly, crudely, without qualifying clauses. I will sketch it in firm black pencil-strokes and put in no shading. If I had only one sermon to preach and wanted to epitomise my belief, this is how I should do it.

God made all the worlds and not merely the earth.

They swing in their orbits without cross-communications. Each globe is self-contained; certainly the earth is. One order of existence at a time is the Divine plan.

On this little globe called the earth, He tries out a great experiment. Progressive development shall be its ruling principle. God will begin with the nearest approach to nothingness, and the final issue shall be found in Man.

The Man himself shall be compact of lowly elements, but shall have also within him the germ of spiritual potency. He shall be dust—and spirit. His feet shall be in the mud, but his head among the stars. He shall be gripped by the heel, as though a serpent entwined its coils about him, but shall have powers of mind and spirit by which he may prevail.

He shall be fully conscious of his failures and defeats, but shall not succumb to them. Within him there shall be a still small voice, reproving and yet exhorting. He shall know the full power of evil—of darkness, nothingness, and godlessness. But he shall not rot in these things. A higher voice shall never cease to call him onward.

When he has finally emerged, he shall be fitted for higher fellowship with his unseen God who called him into being.

There arrives a time when man becomes conscious of these things. As though he had eaten of the fruit of the tree of knowledge, he is aware both of evil and of good. He is also aware of his Creator.

He identifies the upward-calling voice with his God; he associates the downward-calling voice with something that is opposed to God. He supplicates the higher power for assistance. He resists the lower power. That is the beginning of religion.

It is the will of the Higher Power that His struggling creature should receive spiritual amplification. The means used is called Prayer. There is sufficient answer to it to reward man's faith.

He dreams now of the help of God. At first he imagines that this help will come from without. He tries to persuade himself that violent disturbances in Nature are sent for this purpose. Signs in the sun and moon and stars, storms, earthquakes, and parted rivers are among the evidences of the Divine help.

Slowly he discovers that his help comes from within. The soul is fortified by invisible grace—God is within rather than without. He finds his truest help outside himself in God-filled men. He calls them saints, because they embody spiritual grace; prophets, because they see the inner meaning of things. He often misunderstands them, indeed may slay them, but in his heart he reveres them, and places them at last in the niches of his temple of reverence. The children build the tombs of the prophets whom the fathers slew.

God sends the prophets. The secret of their enduement is with Him alone. They are His goads and guides, who keep men from succumbing to the evil that is within them. They strengthen the conscience. They lift the world to greater levels. They bear in their bodies the spear-points of the contending forces of good and evil. God sends them, and is Himself their exceeding great reward.

It is the only way. The purer the saint and the bolder the prophet, the more does God come to man.

No other way is open to Him. His very omnipotence disqualifies Him from using other methods. His power is too great to be unloosed. Were He to display it, men would succumb to God as they are in danger of succumbing to evil. God does not want men to succumb—even to Himself. The Divine will is that men should plod through like a pilgrim; fight through like a soldier.

It is the only way! Yet along that line God can do more. He can and He will send a true saint, a veritable prophet.

We know Him as Jesus. He is the world's true saint, without eccentricities, without weaknesses. He is the world's true prophet, not merely proclaiming coming events, but enforcing everlasting principles.

The secret of His being is with God. As indeed it was with every real saint or prophet. Once we have believed that the redeeming God was in every true saint and prophet, we know that He was even more so in Him. How much more so we cannot define. He Himself said that He was one with God, and we believe Him. It is enough for us.

We try to express it in dogmas. We are out of our depth. We are confused by the twin thoughts of an invisible omnipresent God and a localised man in human form. But the essential thing is to know that God is revealing Himself in the only way that is open to Him.

And what happens now?

This! The age-long conflict is precipitated. Evil comes to its maximum of badness. Good comes to its supreme demonstration as a spiritual force. Evil clenches its fist and smites at the face of God in Him. The Spirit of God is triumphant in the dark hour.

O love of God! O sin of man,
In this dread hour thy strength was tried.
And victory remains with Love!
Jesus, our Lord, was crucified.

It is the Atonement. The At-one-ment. That is to say that God is at one with man in the struggle between the good and the evil, the higher and the lower.

One way only, I have said, has been open to God for the redemption of man without destroying his moral integrity. He can by His spirit enter the heart of man, amplifying his powers in the conflict with evil. His choicest approach has been through inspired personality. Every saint and prophet has been a partial incarnation. The Good Spirit ever aims at His own embodiment in personality. Man's tragedy has been not to recognise God when He drew near in such appearances. It has seemed again and again that He has forsaken His prophets in their hour of trial. Why has their lot been so hard? It has been all along a redemption by sacrifice—by blood, as the Bible says. It must always be so. Even now, if men died out who were willing to suffer that their fellows might be saved, the downward pull would overmatch the upward pull.

Here God bears witness that all these sacrificial lives were emanations from His own being, and now by a supreme giving of One who was so like Himself that men have believed He transcended ordinary humanity; so full of Himself that God stood revealed. He bears witness that He takes in Himself the full penalty of evil.

He has made the world subject to evil, not as a thing apart from Himself, but as something in which He shares. Down in its deepest darkness He can forgive. Out of the depths of sin He can redeem. God is at-one with man.

How we have disfigured this high doctrine! How faulty and how crude have been our metaphors and similes! Some of them have justly enough been called, by a recent writer, "an intellectual nightmare."

Maybe! So far as the explanation goes, they deserve to be called so. But the thing itself is of overwhelming beauty and of amazing power. Even under defective images, the imprisoned truth has been powerful. If once let wholly free, it could save the world.

God is at-one with man in the struggle of the higher with the lower. His subjection of the creation to pain and travail and vanity was not a dark doom flung from His hand, as Jove might fling the thunderbolts. It is God in man, striving, suffering, triumphing in the conflict with evil.

Sinners only are doomed if they persist in succumbing. They who have deeply sinned are the more welcome when they repent, for grace can now abound. None need despair, for God is at-one with them in every upward endeavour.

The love of God releases the powers of the Spirit. There is only one name for this. It is a Gospel. God's good tidings, "God's spell," as the old folk-word has it.

We fumble for appropriate words. We have worn out the old formulæ. Give us but the living word to bring this truth home to our generation, and we shall see a revival of Christianity.

For nothing else has ever touched the deep need of man like that!

SOUGHT AND SEEKING

REV. JAMES MOFFATT, D.D., D.Litt., Washburn Professor of Church History Union Theological Seminary, New York.

Formerly Professor of Church History; U.F. College, Glasgow, since 1915; *born in Glasgow, July* 4, 1870; *son of the late George Moffatt, C.A., Glasgow; married,* 1896, *Mary, eldest daughter of the late Dr. Arch. Reith, Aberdeen; two sons, one daughter. Educated at the Academy, University, and Free Church College, Glasgow; M.A. (Classical Honours) and John Clark Fellow (Classics), Glasgow University; Stevenson Scholar, Freeland Scholar, (Hebrew), Joshua Paterson Fellow, F.C. College, Glasgow. Ordained* 1896; *Jowett Lecturer, London,* 1907; *Yates Professor of Greek and New Testament Exegesis, Mansfield College, Oxford,* 1911–15. *Publications: "The Historical New Testament," English edit. and transl. of Harnack's "Ausbreitung des Christentums," "The Golden Book of Owen," "Literary Illustrations of the Bible," "Primer to Novels of George Meredith," Editions of Thessalonians and Revelation in "Expositor's Greek Testament," "Paul and Paulism," "Critical Introduction to New Testament Literature," "Theology of the Gospels," New Translation of the New Testament; "The Approach to the New Testament" (Hibbert Lectures).*

SOUGHT AND SEEKING

BY THE REV. PROFESSOR JAMES MOFFATT

"I have gone astray like a lost sheep; seek Thy servant; for I do not forget Thy commandments."—Ps. cxix. 176.

THAT is the last word of a long psalm, a very long psalm. And what a strange last word it is! You expect something by way of a climax or a crescendo. Most of the psalms end upon a clear, ringing note of assurance and confidence, or leave us in a rapture. They may begin low, but they commonly rise and close upon higher ground. Whereas this psalm seems to die away in a wistful, humble cry of confession: "I have gone astray like a lost sheep." In the Anglican Prayer Book (and there is no change in the revised edition) such a confession comes at the beginning of the service: "We have erred, and strayed from Thy ways like lost sheep." Here it is the crowning word of all the pleas and cries that have preceded.

> I have gone astray like a lost sheep;
> seek Thy servant;
> for I do not forget Thy commandments.

A strange ending, and yet one that sounds very honest. It is the pleading of a man who is trying to tell the truth about himself, neither extenuating nor exaggerating the facts. He does not minimise what he has done. Yet neither does he make himself out to be worse than he really is. And sometimes people do that. Exaggeration is one of the vices of our religious vocabulary, for we are constantly tempted to use swollen language about our souls and perhaps unconsciously to overstate things. To hear some folk talk, for example, about a person who has gone wrong, one would imagine that they had never been tempted at all. They speak of the scandal from such a lofty height of superior virtue that they convey the impression of living far above the common risks and frailties of human nature. Others, again, may accuse themselves of all manner of evil in a heat of self-reproach; they charge themselves loudly, till, as we listen, we feel that they cannot surely be as bad as they make out. This is, no doubt, a nobler habit than the other. Still, however generous and faithful, it is apt to become unreal; and we ought to be real, honest, and accurate in speaking of ourselves to God or to our fellow-men. There is always something impressive and convincing about a man who does not spare himself but who at the same time does not try to paint himself blacker than he really is. "I have gone astray," says the psalmist; "I've been stupid, I've got myself into a wrong position, I'm in danger." He blames nobody else for his plight. He is too honest to talk of circumstances, but owns up frankly to his personal responsibility for having got off the right track. But then he is not content to remain where he is. "Seek Thy servant," he adds at once, "for I do not forget Thy commandments." Conscience tells him that he is meant to be under the orders of God instead of obeying his own impulses or following the crowd. I have forgotten myself, he means, but I have not quite forgotten the true end of life; I have still some sense of the will of God and some desire to regain the straight road.

Such is the right view to take of our faults: without being lax, we ought to take them quietly; we must not allow ourselves to be overwhelmed, or to imagine that everything is lost. No one who is flippant or superficial would say, "I have gone astray like a lost sheep." But there is no use in being cast down, as though we had dropped too far for recovery. The first instinct ought to be that our lives are still within reach of God. "Seek Thy servant." When a lapse comes, when we have given way to some temptation, and failed badly, there should be an instant sense that we are out of our right place. We belong to God; we have no business to be where we are; we have landed ourselves in a false position by yielding to our lower impulses. "I think," says Walt Whitman in one of his wild outbursts, "I could turn and live with animals, they are so placid and self-contained. They do not sweat and whine about their condition; they do not lie awake in the dark and weep for their sins." No, for they are animals and not human beings. And we are more than animals. We are not sheep, but we are like sheep when we sink below ourselves. Conceivably we might bring ourselves to rest content with the life of mere impulse and placid, natural desire. If we did not remember who we are and whom we promised to serve, there would be no dissatisfaction at all. But there is. And as we feel a grievance against ourselves for having sunk to a lower level, it is a positive encouragement; for it means that our faults and failures have not yet stifled the sense of life's true end and aim. "I do not forget Thy commandments."

> Oh, we're sunk enough here, God knows,
> But not quite so sunk that moments,
> Sure though seldom, are denied us,
> When the spirit's true endowments

Stand out clearly from its false ones,
And apprise it if pursuing
Or the right way or the wrong way
To its triumph or undoing.

Perhaps most people tend to take their faults far too lightly nowadays. There is a reaction against the stress on sin which characterised the religion of the last generation in its evangelical aspect. The emphasis has shifted. Indeed if we look farther back, one striking contrast emerges between our modern age and the period which we call the Middle Ages. On the whole mediæval folk, so far as they were religious, were preoccupied with sin and strangely indifferent to suffering ; they seem to have been much more sensitive to offences against God than to the pain endured by their fellow-creatures. Nowadays it is the opposite. The modern conscience is extremely sensitive to pain, even sensitive to the point of sentimentalism, but it is not nearly so alive to sin. The present age is by no means so callous to certain forms of suffering in the world as the Middle Ages often were, but it has nothing like the acute consciousness of sin as sin. The average person to-day is not greatly cast down by faults and failings, not sobered when he goes wrong, not moved to be thoughtful and penitent.

Yet, on the other hand, some are still deeply moved. Generalisations are misleading things, and under the surface of life to-day there are still a number of people who secretly are almost crushed by the sense of their unsteadiness, and apt to be depressed by their breakdowns, till they may feel that it is little use for them to try to be religious any longer, when the will seems so easily twisted to evil and bent to lower things. Some of you may feel this, or may know some who are in this desperate position, either through some sharp, definite failure, or through the slow accumulation of things which have silted up like sand and covered the nobler aspirations of the past. It is the position in which one feels that one has taken such liberties with oneself in the body or in the spirit that one has departed from the living God. For some reason or another the clean mind, the honest heart, the straight discipline of the religious life, are practically memories ; and one wakens suddenly to the sense of this. A moment of insight arrives, when in a flash the contrast between what we are and what we were meant to be stands out before our startled eyes. It is not a morbid mood, not to be pooh-poohed as an unhealthy feeling. But neither are we to yield to it as final.

The true word for us in such a mood is the word of this old psalmist, who plainly was facing just such an experience. Instantly he turns from his faults to God. " Seek Thy servant," he cries, " for I do not forget Thy commandments." You see, it is not only that we desire to get back, but that there is One who seeks to have us back. It is something to be conscious that, in spite of what has happened, we still remember the true end of life. But it is more, it is everything, to feel that our wistful desire to regain the right track is only the echo of God's desire to have us back. We are His sheep, His servants. That is, the meaning of life lies in our relation to Another, not in self-gratification or self-interest ; and our lingering consciousness of this is the outcome of the working of God's Spirit still within us. The saving thing is this sense that we are still wanted by Him. As Mr. A. C. Benson put it, " As soon as one realises that, one is on the right track ; because not only does one know that one is seeking something, but one becomes aware of a much larger fact, that one is being sought by Some One else, sought, not as a dog may trace a wounded creature through the grass and lose the scent at last, but sought patiently and faithfully."

This is what Jesus came to do and comes to do, to "go after that which is lost till He finds it." That curious twinge of conscience, that uneasiness of mind after you have committed a fault, that sense of inward shame, that self-reproach, that restless feeling—that is God stirring you up! It means that you are not being left to yourself. The Lord to whom you belong is seeking you out till He brings you to your right mind again. He will not let you go. He needs you in His service still. Life does not leave you face to face with your past, your weak, bad past. No, no! Even in that far-off age the psalmist knew better than to imagine such a thing. And now that Jesus has come, we should know better still. There is One coming in search of us, to put us back into our right place in His service and fellowship. "Seek Thy servant," is our cry, when we are moved to the depths. And the answer from the heights of heaven is this: "As a shepherd seeketh out his flock in the day that he is among his sheep that are scattered abroad, so will I seek out My sheep; I will seek that which is lost, and will bind up that which is broken, saith the Lord God."

Such is the promise and power of the Lord for you and for me, in our faulty, unsteady lives, so forgetful of His orders, so easily swerving from His care and control. We make slips, pretty bad slips. We give way to temptation. We are wilful, stupid creatures;

we fail deplorably. Well, but are we not living in a year of the Lord, and in a world full of forgiveness, where He is ever following up His people to set them right again and to restore them ? " Seek Thy servant ! " Lord, Thou knowest we are poor servants, and sometimes not servants of Thy will at all. But we are meant to be, and, despite all that has happened, we mean to be.

So it comes to this. It is a real thing, this failure of yours, this shameful collapse, a fault not to be hidden or ignored. Yes, but this is real too, the seeking Lord, the Lord coming to you at once and never ceasing till He finds you and has you back in His service. He misses you, as well as you miss Him. If you wish one of the shortest and most hopeful prayers of penitence, say to yourself, or rather say to God, " I have gone astray like a lost sheep—a silly creature ; seek Thy servant, for I do not quite forget Thy commandments." I think that is one of the best pillow-texts in the Bible. You can rest on it with an honest and a good conscience, and waken to-morrow morning better able to keep straight and to be more obedient.

Cancelled from
Gladstone's Library
13 MAR 2023
GLADSTONE'S
LIBRARY

Printed in Great Britain by
Hazell, Watson & Viney Ld.
London and Aylesbury
F30.228